WEAVING
THE
THREADS

Discovering the Patterns of our Lives: 1922 - 2012

Edited by

Enid Baron & Barbara Gazzolo

CONTENTS

Preface xi

Acknowledgments xiii

Introduction xv

Dedication xix

THEMES

PART ONE: BEGINNINGS

Penelope Whiteside
SEPARATE THREADS 3

Ruth Sherman
IN THE BEGINNING 9

Ruth Granick
BROOKLYN HEIGHTS 11

Pat Lee
CONFESSIONS OF A COUNTRY SCHOOL TEACHER 15

Lou Polley
THE GREAT DEPRESSION 19

Ruth Sherman
LIVING IT UP 21

Barbara Gazzolo
PHILIP 23

Beata Hayton
CABOOSE CHILD 25

Pat Lee
FAINTING 29

Helen Levy
SCHNECKLE 33

Enid Baron
FIRST LOVE... 35

PART TWO: FAMILY MATTERS

Ruth Sherman
PROBLEM SOLVING IS WHAT IT'S ALL ABOUT 43

Penelope Whiteside
MYTHIC CHILDHOOD 45

Dorothy Chaplik
OF BOOKS AND BICYCLES 49

Deanne Thompson
BRAIDS.. 53

Ruth Granick
MOTHER RUSSIA.. 55

Sarah Mirkin
MY AUNT MARGARET PLAYED THE PIANO 59

Ruth Sherman
MY INHERITANCE 63

Deanne Thompson
AUNT ALICE 65

Diane Ciral
WHAT'S FOR LUNCH? 67

Stella Mah
THE WAR YEARS IN CHUNKING 69

Helen Levy
THE HABERDASHER WHO SAVED THE FAMILY 73

Sarah Mirkin
SAILING WITH BERNARD 75

Ruth Sherman
ANYTHING FOR THE KINDER (CHILDREN)....................83

PART THREE: HARD TIMES

Ruth Sherman
GROWING UP THE HARD WAY 87

Lou Polley
THE WAR..91

Stella Mah
LEAVING CHINA (PARTS I AND II).......................93

Nancy Braund-Boruch
THE BOX 99

Deanne Thompson
CHICAGO PARK CITY 101

Pat Lee
ONE SUMMER DAY 103

Ruth Granick
HANS FELL...105

Lou Polley
AN INCREDIBLE JOURNEY 107

Barbara Gazzolo
MARY...109

Penelope Whiteside
PELICANS 113

PART FOUR: MAPPING
THE WORLD

Stella Mah
A WHOLE NEW WORLD 117

Beata Hayton
COLLEGE AND WAY BEYOND 121

Mary Lee Maloney
OMOSHIROI NEE (INTERESTING, ISN'T IT?) 125

Deanne Thompson
FISHING TRIP 129

Helen Levy
MELALINDA 131

Pat Lee
AN AUSTRALIAN EXPERIENCE 133

Mary Lee Maloney
NEW YORK, NEW YORK 139

Beata Hayton
FIRE! 143

Diane Ciral
KIM 145

Mary Lee Maloney
CLOSE CALL 147

Diane Ciral
THANKSGIVING 153

Sarah Mirkin
FINISHING NYANSHA 155

PART FIVE: WEAVING THE THREADS

Penelope Whiteside
SCRUBBING CARROTS ON A SUNDAY MORNING........165

Ruth Granick
ME AND MY CHURCHES 169

Barbara Gazzolo
TRAVELS WITH ADELE 175

Sarah Mirkin
WHOSE STUFF IS THIS ANYWAY? 181

Stella Mah
DURIAN 185

Lou Polley
THE BEST TIMES OF OUR LIVES.........................187

Barbara Gazzolo
MY NAME IS ALBERT 189

Mary Lee Maloney
THE AMERICAN DREAM TURNED RANCID 191

Diane Ciral
STUDS TERKEL 195

Dorothy Chaplik
FATHER AND SON...197

Penelope Whiteside
HYMN 663 203

Ruth Granick
I GROW OLD 207

Contributors 209

Mary Lee Maloney
CLOSING DEDICATION TO RUTH................................ 219

PREFACE
by Barbara Gazzolo

This summer I celebrated my eightieth birthday. Eighty candles were scattered on five cakes. It makes you sit up and take notice. Where have I been? Where did the time go? What has my life meant? Writing one's memoirs helps answer these life questions, helps round life out.

When we nine women first gathered at Evanston's Levy Senior Center for a memoir–writing class, we had no intention of making a book. We may have been trying to make sense of our lives, or at the very least push ourselves to leave a record for posterity, but over the course of the four years we became sisters. You can't share significant parts of your life with others without bonding in a special way. I would look forward to Tuesday, even when I had trouble choosing or even recovering a memory of interest. I would go to bed on Monday night at times wondering what to write for the next day. Writing was always easier for me than retrieving memory. That's part of my aging, I guess.

The process of writing our memoirs had two faces. As we shared them in class, we grew closer to each other, but perhaps of more importance we came to understand our own selves better. Reflecting on our lives is important work in these later years. This is the time we have been given to knit it all together and listen for its melody.

When I first joined the class it was with the intention of spurring myself to write an account of a correspondence with a man serving a life sentence in Menard Correctional Center, a high–security facility in Illinois. I was able to record some of my correspondence with Derek but, as I did so, other pieces of *my* life history began to claim attention and ask for their place. When you engage in writing memoirs, you rediscover the life you have lived. Things come back to you, and sometimes you see new meaning in it all. Our class would grow and shrink, but many of us have stayed together these four years. We have been enriched by writing and hearing each others' stories, and I see those eighty candles on my cakes now with new appreciation.

If you were to encounter one of us from the memoir class on the street, you would hardly mark our presence. We are "ordinary" women of a certain age. We move rather slowly, our hair is gray, but we have lived long and lived to write our stories. Our writing has improved over the years and though we never intended to produce a book, it seemed a shame not to share the humor and wisdom that have emerged.

There is a place for stories such as ours in this culture. The lessons of history are not widely taught anymore, and the culture in which we live makes a fetish of youthfulness—its freshness, energy, and beauty. Nevertheless, the young will always need mentoring and need to learn from the wisdom and mistakes of their elders. Civilizations mature when history is heeded. The memoirs of these ordinary women can serve as mentoring, enabling readers to revalue the wisdom that comes from life's lessons.

ACKNOWLEDGMENTS

Thanks to Leslie Wilson, program director of the Levy Senior Center of Evanston, Illinois, who for the last four years has provided us with a sunny space in the library on Tuesday afternoons. Also, our thanks to Christina Ferraro, senior services manager at the Levy Center, and the members of the Life Enrichment Fund for their interest and support. To Bill Rattner of Lawyers For The Creative Arts for his invaluable counsel.

To Linda Stone, author of the mystery *What's Going on at the Montcliff?*, who has always been there to offer her knowledge and experience in the world of publishing, many thanks. To Ellen Wade Beals, editor of the anthology *Solace in So Many Words*, a big thank–you for her guidance and advice. We also thank Donald J. Berk, author of *In Search of Wings Lost*, and Larry Wardell, author of *Confessions of a Closet Yogi*, for their counsel and time. Our appreciation to Helen Gallagher, author of the best-selling *Release Your Writing: Book Publishing, Your Way*.

Lee Blum, PhD, therapist, teacher, and dear friend, recommended *The Redemptive Self*, written by her colleague Dan McAdams, PhD, chairman of the Clinical Psychology Program of the Department of Psychology at Northwestern University. Special thanks to Dr. McAdams for taking the time to confer with us about his research. Thanks also to communications expert Robin Schuette, who advised us about the format and costs of producing this book. Kate Sloane Fiffer, publishing consultant, spent many hours explaining the uses of social networking.

Marjorie Price, painter, graphic designer, and author of the memoir *A Gift from Brittany*, has been an invaluable resource in our design concept. Thanks to Jack Weiss, graphic designer, whose talent and patient counsel inspired our cover, and to Faigie and Robert Tanner, photographers, who went out of their way to work with us on cover design. Sandra Ullmann, psychologist and photographer, made her work available to us and offered invaluable advice. Thanks, also, to her husband, Tom Ullmann, whose counsel and encouragement we cherish. And to Elias Turner for finding our cover photograph.

A special acknowledgement to Carol LaChapelle, a pioneer in the field of memoir whose book *Finding Your Voice, Telling Your Stories* is an invaluable resource for those who wish to record their life stories.

To Chelsea Olive Lord, without whose computer skills, patience, and good judgment this book would never have been completed; and to Lindy Rubin, arts educator, for her generosity in connecting us with Chelsea. To Cynthia Percak Serikaku, copyeditor above and beyond our expectations, whose eagle eyes found the errors and polished this manuscript to a shining gloss; and to fellow writer Mary Driver-Thiel, who led us to Cindy.

Most of all, we thank and acknowledge the Levy Center Memoir Class, whose finely crafted life stories have inspired this book. A special thanks to class members Stella Mah and Sarah Mirkin for keeping us on track and solvent. And to Diane Ciral, whose organizational skills and pragmatism saved us countless hours.

Finally, this anthology is dedicated to the memory of Ruth Sherman, whose courage, humor, and heart endeared her to us all. Many thanks to her husband, Bob Sherman, for his encouragement and support of this project.

INTRODUCTION
by Enid L. Baron, PhD

It wasn't very long ago that memoirs were written by those whose stars hung in the firmament of fame. So-called ordinary people couldn't think of a good reason for writing their life stories. We took it for granted that our lives were like everyone else's. Nothing special, we thought.

On second thought, after a death in the family, we may have stumbled on topsy-turvy photo albums in dusty attics or at the back of a closet. Even when someone's name had been scrawled along the border of a photo, the writing was often impossible to make out. And what about those shoeboxes containing old letters, some of which were bound with satin ribbons. Love letters? Did we have the right to read them, we wondered? We had no qualms about reading the manifolds of ships that carried our ancestors across the Atlantic during the great migrations at the turn of the century. So many names changed at Ellis Island, it was a wonder that we recognized our family at all. But there they were.

Let us consider our families of origin: parents, grandparents, great-grandparents, as far back as we can go. Occasionally we think we've struck gold with a diary a grandmother kept about her life before she met Grandpa. We open it eagerly only to find trivia about parties, refreshments, who danced with whom. But what about the later events of their lives: babies born one after another, people struggling to keep them fed and bathed and clothed, especially after World War I broke out and the young husband sent overseas?

They are gone now. Who will answer our questions? "Dear Aunt Rosa, Do you remember the name of the town in Italy where Grandpa was born?" or "Dear Cousin Sophie, Is it true that we had a great-uncle who was a general in the Russian Revolution?" or "Dear Mom, Whatever happened to that cut-glass bowl you used to fill with fruit and use as a centerpiece on the dining room table? I've looked for it everywhere."

We have lived through World War II, Korea, Viet Nam, Iraq, and Afghanistan. Our families have sustained terrible losses. Whose life could ever be ordinary after losses like those? Who will be left to tell our grandchildren about the day we gathered around the radio to hear President Roosevelt announce the attack on Pearl Harbor? Or how we filled our wagons with bundles of old newspapers, which we dragged to school for the war effort? Or watching our big sisters draw seams on the backs of their bare legs, when nylon was requisitioned for the manufacture of parachutes? Air–raid drills that sent us scuttling in twos out of our classrooms and down into the school basement until the all-clear signal sounded? How our families passed around those thin, blue V-mail letters from Europe with trembling hands?

When finally the war was over, America found itself in the boom times of a postwar economy and the country went crazy over television, even though the black–and–white images seemed to be fighting their way through snow. But tragedies continued. No one will ever forget what he or she was doing on the day President Kennedy was assassinated. Or erase the image of Jacqueline Kennedy following her husband's cortège through Washington's streets, holding her little childrens' hands? The assassination of Dr. Martin Luther King Jr.?

Despite these hard times, we also remember building forts from mounds of snow after the great blizzard of 1968 when schools were closed and cars could not be navigated on the streets. Summer vacations in a tiny cabin in Wisconsin, where we watched the sun set every night and built bonfires on the beach. Holding our first child in our arms. Our first grandchild.

Because of our memoirs, future generations will have the opportunity to know us through our own voices. Our stories will heighten their sense of identity at a time in which personal history may have become devalued and when the complexities of a global world make it increasingly important to have a strong sense of the world as it once was and our kin who occupied it.

Among his many contributions to our understanding of the human condition, psychiatrist Erik Erikson, in his book *Childhood and Society*, identifies eight stages of life. According to Erikson, each stage holds the possibility of a positive or a negative outcome, depending on how it is negotiated.

Many of today's memoirists, as in the case of the authors of *Weaving the Threads*, are in their seventies and eighties, the stage Erikson terms Ego Integrity versus Ego Despair. Ego Integrity represents the ability to see our lives as a unified whole. By reviewing the obstacles we've faced and the challenges we've met, we are better able to forgive our failures and appreciate our accomplishments. One memory leads to another and before we know it, we have discovered that our memory banks are loaded with riches, stories long forgotten, and stories that may have been told and even re-told but never recorded for posterity. We are astonished at what rich and full lives we have led. As the author and memoirist Patricia Hampl has said, "We write our stories to listen to what they tell us."

For many of us, it is the first time in our lives that we have the time and opportunity to look back at the journey we've taken, not necessarily in a chronological pattern but as memory gives way to memory, story to story. Equipped with enhanced insights and a sense of satisfaction, we are able to move forward to explore new options, blaze new trails, take on new challenges.

DEDICATION

Ruth Nelson Sherman
1931-2011

"Don't I know you from 14 years ago?"
"Does your aunt still suffer from a skin condition?"
"I have a great dermatologist for her!"
"Did I tell you about the Rabbi from Kiev?"

I have just encapsulated what my wife represented:
A fantastic memory
A solution for everyone
A great sense of humor

I was fortunate enough to be married to Ruth for 53 years. As I said at the funeral, it was 52 ½ of the best years of my life. If you take the six months that were a problem and divide it by 53, I only got aggravation 3 days a year.

Ruth had a driving force that we should all have. Survival is the key word. Born during the Great Depression to new immigrants from the "Old Country," Yiddish was the first language she learned. Her father never caught on with the modern world and her mother was a frightened woman who did not know how to live with a problem husband and a young child. Yet love remained in the house.

How many, at the age of 19, would realize that life in the Bronx would stifle her? With $54 in her pocket, Ruth bought a $34 ticket to Chicago, hoping to stay there for a few months and allowing her to earn some money so she could continue on to the west coast. Arriving at Midway Airport, she asked a cab driver where she could get housing and he took her to the YMCA. The next day she went to the Jewish Vocational Office and said, "Here I am! Get me a job!"

From that point on, she caught a break and met me! However, she already gathered a bevy of friends who adored her. That was the type of person she was. I was blown away, never having met such a self-sufficient person. To make a long story short, because she covers a lot of this in her memoirs, at age 40, Ruth decided to go to college and get the degree she never had a chance to get when she was younger. This is while she was raising two girls and taking care of a needy husband.

Somehow she accomplished all this and proceeded to work as a social worker for over 23 years. All during this period her only interest was helping people. I am thrilled that she instilled such great traits in both our daughters. Also, her qualities have filtered down to her three grandkids, who were the light of her life.

If you met Ruth, you were enriched. I cannot express what she meant to me. Read her memoirs and you will get a feel of what Ruth is. Read the memoirs from others and you may understand the joy she received by being associated with the writers in her memoir class. The world is sadder without Ruth, but it is richer because of her.

—BOB SHERMAN

BEGINNINGS

SEPARATE THREADS
by Penelope Whiteside

One of my favorite college classmates wrote in our fiftieth college reunion book about the tapestry of her life, of all that she had never dreamed of but had happened anyways! I was intrigued by her image. I also reflected on the weaving of that tapestry. How is it, I wondered, that so many separate threads meet in one life. How do all those separate pieces finally come together. I'm not sure I have the answer. Perhaps there are multiple personalities and possibilities within all of us. I, for one, am working on pulling all of the threads together. At what point does the pattern of oneself become evident?

I confess that building alternative universes is an old indulgence of mine. Fantasy has always been a welcome escape from the examined life, the purposeful understanding of those various colored threads that have created the pattern that is uniquely mine. Memory provides only a fragile nexus. Those earlier selves can appear as familiar strangers, not as friends of my own choosing. I've determined to sit at my loom, though. My name is Penelope, after all! Perhaps I can at least start to identify the colors of those threads that make up my personal tapestry.

I start with my earliest memories. The baby thread is the color of a brownish-blue afternoon. At twenty-two months, I am stretching my arms up as high as I can to reach the mattress of my new brother's crib, the one so lately mine. There is a tall woman in a white uniform who is allowing me to help put the sheet on. My room down the hall has a new twin bed. One day, I climbed the radiator in that room and fell off, bringing the family doctor. He was a kind man who squatted beside my crying self. I had imaginary friends in that room: Meat Mommie, Boy, and a white-garbed figure with white eyeballs who scared me. I called her Ree. Much of my life before two was spent in my room. My mother would declare her strategy to passing guests: "Penny comes out for 'social hour' at 5 p.m." I wonder what they thought. As my brother grew into a happy, slobbering baby, I seemed to grow cranky. At least I seem to be scowling in most of the pictures taken of me back then. There is one where I'm smiling. I'm looking up over an open book. Someone must have read me a story.

The threads from the elementary school years are yellow. Yellow for the color of my best friend Carol's hair and the color of the school bus that took us to Center School where I loved to be, for the optimism I felt around my teachers even in that ancient nineteenth-century building with its high windows and its carved wooden desks anchored to the floor by black metal shanks, even for that asphalt play yard where I skinned my knees darting away from the ball that might catch me as we played Relievio. I've forgotten the rules of that game, but I remember the peasant-style polkas that we girls whirled to inside after lunch.

At twelve, I dressed in forest-green jumpers and Peter Pan blouses for boarding school. Green is what I think of for St. Margaret's. I was unaware at first of what a hick was. The first morning at Miss Bailey's table, I ordered not only oatmeal, but scrambled eggs and bacon and toast and orange juice for myself, hardly believing my release from the cold cereal and banana that comprised the usual breakfast at home. Of course, I couldn't eat it all. Miss Bailey disapproved of waste. I had much to learn. A kind classmate of mine gave me my first bra. I had come with undershirts. I knew nothing about grooming. There was much to learn besides the usual school subjects. The green of the jumper was a severe sort of green, but the color of growth nonetheless. Green was the color of those teen years.

A lighter palette started to show itself the summer between high school and college. There was the light of the sparkling mica in the sand at Martha's Vineyard, the leaping orange of camp fires on the beach, the stars above us as we drove down the country roads in an open jeep, the pastels of the light summer skirts we wore to the community square dances. That summer just before college, I felt young, truly young in a magical way. Those days were white and silver.

The colors of college were nuanced, like an impressionist painting by Monet, ever changing with the light. At times they were bright like those that adorned the Venus by Botticelli. I, like Venus, was emerging, gazing beyond the cloistered landscape of my childhood. I was in awe of everything I heard in class and around dining tables. I walked around the campus lake with my first love, even writing my father about the purity of ideals. I smile as I think of how good it was, of how ironic it is that the very emergence of individuality seems to follow such a predictable pattern. For those years I think I would choose mottled shades of thread, with flashes of gold . . .

Three years to the month after college graduation, I was married. Those intervening years were the warp and woof of my tapestry. Interwoven were the exhilarating moments when my first paychecks spelled "freedom," the dreadful awareness that I had not a clue as to where I was headed, that life was already slipping away. My trip down the aisle was both the culmination of a whirlwind romance and another demonstration of my mother's total control of any project, including her daughter's wedding. Her own mother had died when she was fourteen. My wedding was make-up time. Her own bridesmaids—and she invited all seven of them—respectfully declined to enter her fantasy.

Our early marriage was the color of the open road, its azure-white skies, its yellow candlelit dinners. The following year, we added the blue of baby boy clothes and the white of Johnson's baby powder. Bob's friends shared an ochre strand. Most of them were at least ten years older than I and far more sophisticated. They forgave me my obvious lack of worldliness. What else could you do with someone who offered peanut butter and jelly sandwiches among the samovars at Ravinia. My picnics were strictly country.

White was surely the first color of my early nursing years—the white stockings and dress of the hospital in the 1980s, the lab coats of later forays into student health at the local university and blood collection for LifeSource. There was the yellow-and-green of the old

"L" cars that bore me, still doing my homework, to the Soviet-style buildings where I obtained a master's degree in public health.

After thirty years of marriage, the unthinkable happened. There were the subdued aqua tones of hospital corridors. The husband who was supposed to last a lifetime sickened and died. Grief and rage came in red and blue.

Within the year-and-a-half following Bob's death I had traveled twice—first to Israel where the colors of a desert landscape mingled with the tree-clad hills of Galilee. Next, I joined a mission to India. The saffrons, bright fuchsia silks, the dusty browns of Calcutta streets, the cool gray-white of the Taj Mahal jumped into my fabric, transforming me utterly. I was alert as never before. American streets are restfully monotonous compared to the byways of Bombay, Varanasi, and Calcutta. Strands of spirit wove themselves in.

My second husband was also named Bob. He entered my life in the afternoon light of my back porch. He came with an old friend of his and a college classmate of mine. After boxed wine—I was the country hick once again, I fear—we retired to a dimly lit vegetarian restaurant where the food was mediocre but the liveliness at table was lit by an orange flame. There were the anxious colors of impatience, too, as this new Bob traveled, first to Europe and then to Japan. One day, a postcard arrived with bright red and blue umbrellas. It was from Bob. The spirit of exhilaration, of infatuation, had seized him as well. We were married the following summer. I can hardly tell which colors pertained to my new life. They whizzed past, silver, like those planes we caught so frequently to London, Rome, and Berlin, to San Francisco and New York. They were also blue like Lake Leggo and Lake Wansee, bright red-orange like the Tucson poppies, pastel like the houses perched on California hillsides. Alas, all too soon, there was the black of an early December morning when this Bob also died.

I stopped collecting threads for my tapestry for a while. It was enough to put one foot in front of another. I traveled again. South Africa and China offered whole new worlds, as did in a lamentable way, Haiti. I continued to fly. Airplanes were more like buses to me now, less like eagles.

The task of weaving together these strands of life remains before me. Will I add still more threads? Perhaps I will be content merely to gaze at the present world of park and garden. At college reunion last week, I and my friends from fifty years ago asked, "Where has the time gone?" We regretted not having taken advantage of all our college had to offer while we were there. In the end, though, we sighed collectively and forgave ourselves. "We were so young," we said. Those familiar strangers, the selves I once inhabited, do need forgiveness after all. They are all there. The trick, I guess, is to gather the wisdom of passing years, and to keep on weaving.

IN THE BEGINNING
by Ruth Sherman

Mama met Papa on a park bench in Eastern Parkway in Brooklyn. This was sometime in the late 1920s, and they were there with their respective friends.

Mama was in her late twenties, and the family was concerned about her lack of marital status. So that day on the park bench, Mama made a big mistake. She ended up talking to Papa. Not too long afterward they got married, and I cannot say they lived happily ever after.

They went on a traditional honeymoon to Lakewood, New Jersey and, in their hotel room, Mama realized that she had made a big mistake. To begin with, Papa's luggage, when opened, revealed a large pink rubber bag prominently displayed on top. *"Vot iss diss, Yudel?"* she queried, to which Papa replied, *"Id iss mine klisteer und I dun go novere vidoud id"* (It's my enema bag and I don't go nowhere without it).

Slowly the story unfolded, or should I say unraveled.

Papa was a poor Brownsville boy who had recently emigrated from a small shtetl in Poland. As soon as the ship hit Ellis Island, Grandpa Zalman was whisked away to a protected setting. Or, as referred to by the family, a booboo hatch. Papa lived in a heatless, airless tenement flat along with his mother, a tiny toothless woman who spoke no English, and his siblings—a couple of full siblings and a couple of halves. They had no funds except Jewish Home Relief. All the kids found jobs while Baba Basha stayed home and cooked, and cleaned, and whistled through her toothless gums.

Papa had no discernible skills so even the most meager jobs were not available to him. At that time in American history, anyone could get a job no matter how humble. It was said of him that he did not present well. He had tended to the chickens on their shtetl but, when he sought work in the kosher poultry shop on Pitkin Avenue, even the chickens rejected him, squawking loudly when he came near.

Bathing was relegated to once a week, on Shabbas and, because of his birth order in the family, he was the last to bathe in the water that had already been used by five others.

Even chickens have their standards.

BROOKLYN HEIGHTS
by Ruth Granick

When I was nine years old, Fanny and Lou Harris, my aunt and uncle, found a large airy apartment in Brooklyn Heights, and my mother, Clara, and I moved in with them. We had the back area, a lovely, large living room that served as mother's bedroom, and my smaller bedroom, away in a corner, very private. There was a wonderful skylight in the bathroom; it was like a fairyland. Once Lou came out of the bathroom having sprayed himself with Fanny's Chanel #5. She yelled at him. I giggled.

On Sundays, Fanny and Lou and my mother and I walked across the Brooklyn Bridge into Manhattan, and lunched in Chinatown. Once we saw a Chinese film. Children in the audience ran up and down the aisles playing. No one took umbrage.

I loved the library, which was not far from our apartment. An elderly librarian in a black dress watched me for a while during my first visit and asked whether I wouldn't prefer the children's room. I demurred. I don't remember what book I'd picked up, but she asked me to read a little to her. I did so and was permitted to remain in the adult section.

Aunt Fanny did secretarial work. Lou stayed home and painted. I loved the smell of oil paints and turpentine. Once Lou asked me to pose. I did so, trying very hard not to move although I was just a little girl. When he finished, I asked to see the painting. It was not at all me. He'd just wanted the pose. I'd been his mannequin.

Flippy was their lovely, reddish-brown Cocker Spaniel. How I loved her. I have no idea what their problems were, but Fanny and Lou had frequent shouting matches, while Flippy hid under my bed. Sometimes she jumped on it and peed. Clara warned me to keep silent during their fights. The last one I remember ended with Fanny screaming as though she'd been hurt. Clara rushed in to find that Lou had simply touched Fanny's arm, trying to calm her.

Lou used to call my aunt "Fanny" and touch her derriere. She changed her name to Temeena, which she said was Hebrew for Fanny. Good change, but she never responded to it and finally settled for Frances. I think it was during that time that I decided Ruth was a terrible name. I wanted to be called by my middle name, Louise. Like Fanny, I never responded to my newly chosen name, and I went back to being called Ruth.

It was near Easter when a group of girls confronted me in front of my building, telling me that Father had said that the Jews had killed their Lord. They said I had to convert. Although being Jewish in America was not always fun and I was frequently resentful that my family had foisted this on me, I knew I couldn't convert. I just could not. I said that their Jesus had died thousands of years before I was even born, but the girls said they had to fight me. We put our books down. I was terrified. I was nine or ten years old and wouldn't even play ball because people throw things at each other.

There was no real fight. I slapped a girl at her demand but as lightly as possible. She did the same to me. Afterwards we picked up our books and parted. Every day after school, I would see the gang waiting for me in front of my building. I became more and more tense and upset, hating and fearing the walk home. Finally I told my family. Clara said and did nothing. I'm sure she was upset but, never having learned how to protect herself, she couldn't protect me. Frances asked me the name of the ringleader and I told her. She phoned the girl's mother and told her what was happening. The woman spanked her daughter and told her never to do that again.

I did have some friends. Jimmy Hakim was a gorgeous little boy on whom I had a mad crush. Adelaida was a pretty little girl with long black curls on whom Jimmy had a crush. Lila Couri and I were close friends. We would walk to the Syrian bakery for bread, walk back eating it. She told me we were lucky we'd met as youngsters because when we grew up we'd hate each other. Why? Because she was Syrian and I was Jewish. Her mother had explained to her that Syrians and Jews hate each other.

In our elementary school, two other Jewish kids and I, at the top of our class, were chosen to participate in a statewide spelling bee. I was so excited. Then I came down with the chicken pox and spent the next few weeks itching, trying not to scratch, not even able to read because it was thought that light would hurt my eyes. So much for spelling bees.

When I was finally out of quarantine and able to read again, I bought a paperback copy of Emile Zola's *Nana*. This was the first time Clara ever tried to influence my literary endeavors. She told me it was not appropriate for me, and the book disappeared. I bought another copy and started to read it but it disappeared too. The third time I bought the book, it stayed. The only other time my mother tried to censor my reading was connected with Flaubert's *Madame Bovary*, which was in her own collection. She said I wouldn't understand it. Probably so, but I did enjoy reading it, and *Anna Karenina,* too.

One of the girls on our block, Maggie Hart, became my friend. We'd meet on Mondays for our walk to school and I would tell her about my weekend adventures, how I'd boated or swum over to Russia, how I'd been received like a princess. She didn't believe me.

We met again after I had gotten married. I was taking the subway and saw her on the platform. We recognized each other and talked briefly. She told me she'd married Danny Maitland. I remembered him as a very handsome, sweet lad. Then her train came and we never met again.

CONFESSIONS OF A COUNTRY SCHOOL TEACHER
by Pat Lee

My first teaching experience was at a one-room schoolhouse, Millpond School, on Four Mile Road outside of Grand Rapids, Michigan. There were still many one-room school houses back in 1954. Millpond School was a small, wooden structure, ninety-five years old. It had no pond but nearby there were many apple orchards and out back, in the spring, trilliums grew. The next spring, one of my fourth-grade girls picked a trillium bouquet and presented it to me.

A high school friend of mine was a county music teacher who lived a fair way west of the school. She stopped by every Thursday morning to break our day with music. She would park her much-admired VW Bug by the front door as the children shouted out, "Miss Gerry is coming. Miss Gerry is here."

Thank goodness for Miss Gerry and her music. Even though I would prepare diligently, I often wondered if I could make it through each new day. In fact, at first I was so jittery I would dry heave in my parents' bathroom before leaving for school. I had only a two-year junior college graduation diploma and a newly acquired state teaching certificate. The three-man local school board had hired me anyway. I was twenty years old.

That September, we had an unexpected influx of first graders, eight in all, plus the five second graders and the four kindergartners. With the older children, that gave us thirty-four students at Millpond. The school board wisely hired Mrs. Engle to teach the seventeen young ones for half a day. She and I taught together in that same room without disturbing each other or getting in each other's way. When she went home, I taught the second graders after lunch for an hour, then they too left for the day.

When I began the year, I changed the seating patterns into small class groupings. Fourth graders sat in a straight line right in front of me. Eighth graders were against the windows while the sixth graders huddled midway down our space. The big seventh graders took up the back of the room. And I could spin easily from one group to another. My chair had wheels.

My desk up front was near the tiny library, which had a book shelf, a bench, and space to bring in a chair. One seventh grader, Wills, tall and bright, would finish tasks early. "Go read, Wills . . . the encyclopedias, if you wish." I was probably too inexperienced to figure out a special project for him.

One day the older kids and I squeezed into our little library, and I read to them material about Jonas Salk, who invented polio vaccine. I was excited and wanted to share the significance of this with them. My friends and I had survived worried childhood summers shadowed by adult talk of polio. Most of us knew classmates or acquaintances who had become ill with polio or worse. And, of course, President Roosevelt had been afflicted and paralyzed. The children listened quietly, watching my face. I don't remember their asking questions.

Every day after school, I'd write lesson plans for each class in each subject while I played, over and over, "The Carnival of the Animals" on my little record player, loud as I could bear it. I was "Miss Pat" to those children, and they were my dear first students. We had spelling tests every Friday; we had a hayride in the fall and played baseball in the spring. At Christmas there was the obligatory Christmas program. In the spring we all accepted Mrs. Engle's invitation to spend a long afternoon at her family's cottage.

That spring, builders began tearing up the soil to the east of our school. They were going to build a three-room brick schoolhouse with decent bathrooms. No more, our two little toilet rooms at the back of the room, toilet rooms kept clean by school board men, the same men who lit the fire in a big stove as fall and winter came. I don't remember ever being cold in that room. Our little school had survived nearly one hundred years of fierce Michigan winters. It would soon be gone.

We kept our noses to the grindstone despite the noise of construction. Encouraged by the kindness of the supervising teacher who visited us at least three times that year, I would stand about as the children concluded a lesson, acting calm though jittery inside. I knew she would be reporting to the county superintendent, but she always left me feeling warm and reassured.

The year ended in mid-May, but I decided to stay on each morning for two more weeks and try to teach two of the younger children who struggled so with reading. We worked very hard, but I had little or no experience with remedial reading, and am not sure it helped much. Still, they appeared more content, and I felt some sense of accomplishment, accepting their mothers' smiles and the two quarts of fresh strawberries they gave me for payment.

I felt proud when I was invited back to teach the next year. They even offered me $3,700 to stay, a salary that fully degreed Grand Rapids public school teachers got—much better than the $2,800 from my first year. I was flattered but refused. I had other plans. I wanted to graduate from the University of Michigan, get my degree and, when my boyfriend finished school, marry him.

I don't know when the old schoolhouse was demolished. I left quickly, engrossed in preparing for an eight-week summer session in Ann Arbor. I knew Millpond school would be gone but didn't think about it then. I think more about it now and wonder just when it was leveled, and who was there to see it fall. Did anyone salvage a little piece of wood, or a desk or chair? Did Wills come back and take an encyclopedia or two?

I did make a small album of that year and have it still. It's a little six- by nine-inch hard-covered book whose black pages hold pictures of the school's front facade, class groupings, and little individual shots of each face. I know one seventh grader still lives east across the grass and has for many years run an auto repair shop. He would be about sixty-five now. How can that be when I see his young face pictured in front of me?

What of the others? How many stayed in the area? Are most alive? Where did their children go to school? For me, they remain as they were in my small green album. I can imagine them floating among those apple orchards, or perhaps picking springtime trillium, or maybe they search for traces of water that may once have existed, in a place called Mill Pond.

THE GREAT DEPRESSION
by Lou Polley

Born just months after the crash of 1929, during all of my childhood the country was in a severe depression. Thanks to the hard work and sacrifices of my parents, my siblings and I didn't realize it until years later when we read about the Great Depression in our history books.

We were never hungry, our clothes were as nice as everyone else's with lots of home-sewn dresses, shirts, and sunsuits—very popular in the thirties. There was a solid roof over our heads and plenty of coal in the coal chute to last the winter.

The coal chute was actually a room in the basement with a window that opened to the outside and a door that opened to the inside right across from the furnace. On "coal days," our mother would scurry about, tightly closing all the doors and windows so that coal dust would not sift into the rest of the house. We watched excitedly as the big coal truck rattled and banged its way up to the window of the bin. Then one of the workers would shovel coal until the bin was almost full. Usually one delivery would last all winter, for father would bank the coals at night, then stoke them up during the day. This was his way of saving fuel during the depression.

Our father was a staunch Republican who abhorred President Roosevelt's work programs. Father said the WPA stood for "We piddle around and get paid for it."

Our ninety-eight pound mother could take a dollar and stretch it into twenty. When our aunt brought us a live chicken from our grandfather's farm, mother would take the squawking bird out to the back yard and decapitate it with a mighty swoop of a butcher knife. Then she would plunge the bird into hot water and pull off all the feathers. That night we would have fried chicken for dinner, and it was delicious. We never ate out unless it was a picnic, prepared at home and carried to the park. There were no fast-food restaurants in our home town.

We didn't have lots of toys, no TV, video games, or cell phones. In fact, our family got our first phone when my childhood was half over. When we finally got a phone, there were few people to call because few of our friends had phones. When we did call someone, usually our father at work, we would pick up a little receiver and a live voice would say, "Number please." We would SAY the number, and the voice would connect us. We were never bored. A delivery we found exciting, especially on a hot summer day, was the arrival of the iceman carrying a big block of ice for our icebox. Sometimes we would beg a few chips of ice from him, a real treat!

We played outdoors a lot—baseball, softball, hide-and-seek. While I was counting to a hundred, my brother would disappear completely. One day while I was trying to find him, he had ridden off on his bike and broken his arm in three places. Our mother got a call from the hospital. End of game! I later inherited that big old bike that he had fallen from, and it took me weeks to master riding it. "After all," our mother said, "there's no need to buy a bike when we already have one."

I spent hours cutting out and organizing my paper doll collection, clothes, and furniture all chosen from Sears and Montgomery Ward catalogues. And we read. We brought home armloads of books from the library, devoured them, then went back for more. Yes, we were living in the Great Depression, but we didn't know it. We were having too much fun!

LIVING IT UP
by Ruth Sherman

When I was a little girl growing up on the lower East Side, my mama had a very special bribe for me. She would promise to take me to an Italian funeral. Mind you, I did not know these people who had died but had a universal Jewish compassion for all those who had left the Earth. We would dress up in our traditional black *shmatehs* (old clothes) and head over to Second Avenue. We would enter and sit in back seats. Immediately my mama would ask the person next to her, "So, vot side you frum?" After establishing we were from the "other side," we would start to munch on biscotti and fruit.

Another satisfying Italian tea. We really knew how to live it up!

PHILIP
by Barbara Gazzolo

Philip Malcolm was our firstborn son, and to this day he has shaped our family. Not as I would have expected surely, but truly for the better.

When Philip was eighteen months old, I could set him on the red easy chair and go about my business. He would sit there rocking and smiling, blond curls framing his face as he watched me. He never crawled but, on my birthday, I can't remember which one, I brought him into my parents' home and set him on the living room floor amidst the family. I looked around and Philip was on his feet with a look of joy on his face as he reeled across the room. He was over two at the time, and it was his birthday gift to me.

I had taken his slow progress calmly enough, having been told that boys developed less quickly than girls. It's my nature to look on the bright side and besides, his blond curls and happy smile had claimed my heart. But denial exploded one day in the doctor's office when Dr. Earlywine told me I needed to take Philip to Northwestern Memorial Hospital to be evaluated by a well-known neurologist. I recognized the name as the doctor assigned to evaluate the mass murderer Richard Speck. Richard Speck and now my two-year-old blond baby boy.

The day I brought Philip into Northwestern, they gave him an EEG, a brain wave test. They put the little guy on the table and secured his wriggling body in a sheet. I was allowed to be there and asked to help hold him down. As they glued electrodes to his curls, I tried to soothe him.

I spent as much of the day with him as possible, but they wouldn't let me spend the night. My husband had a business dinner date that evening and came for me at the hospital. My heart sank to see Philip in a hospital gown, his tearful face pressed against a window in the door as we left. I will always carry that image in my heart—my frightened child watching me leave. I'm sure I was no asset at the business dinner date. We brought the little guy home the next day, and I can only thank God that hospitals no longer separate a mother from her hospitalized child at night.

Days later I returned to the hospital. Philip and I entered an elevator to see the doctor. Somehow I pressed the wrong floor. Hand-in-hand we stepped out into a very quiet world. The smell of astringents filled the air. No one was around and, through an open door, I believed I saw bodies on tables. Memories are not reliable but even I couldn't have made this up.

My interview with the neurologist was brief. He had no time to waste. There is serious brain damage, I was told, and it was for me to identify what Philip's strengths were and encourage him in that direction. Consultation over. Reeling, I left the doctor's office. I can't remember Philip at my side for this meeting, but I do remember standing in front of the hospital entrance afterwards. It was gray and getting colder. The wind was beginning to blow. I shook my fist at the heavens.

CABOOSE CHILD
by Beata Hayton

I was born when my sister and brother were already going into their teens. My mother remembered Dr. Grotowski, a colleague of my father's, stopping by her hospital room to congratulate her and adding, cheerfully, "All the old women are having babies this year."

Both of my parents were the children of German immigrants. My father, George Mueller, studied pharmacology and was a pharmacist in a Chicago drugstore. The drugstore owner suggested my father might like to try studying medicine. He enrolled at Rush Medical College, which was newly opened, got his MD degree in 1894, and joined the staff of the new St. Mary of Nazareth Hospital on the Northwest Side. In fifty years in practice, he became known for his skill as a surgeon and diagnostician. He was chief of staff at the hospital for a number of years and, when he died, the nuns set his portrait on an easel near the entrance to the hospital chapel with a row of lighted candles in the front.

My mother, Bertha Zaffke, was the oldest of five daughters of a Chicago harness maker and his wife. She worked in an office for a number of years and, after her marriage, she was the family bookkeeper and saw to it that all her children learned to use a typewriter. And she had a great gift for handsome table settings, sometimes seasonal decorations like one I remember with a big round mirror in the center of the table with little china figures of children skating on it.

One summer when we didn't have a cook, I used to get up early and make breakfast for my father, with pancakes, which he liked. My sister, of course, chewed me out for this and said my cooking was no good anyway. Once, I remember, he took me to see a movie at the Granada, and once he took me to see the Cubs play at Wrigley Field. When I was little, a couple of times I went to the hospital with him, and while he saw his patients I visited with the children in the children's ward and the nuns in the kitchen. The nuns said they tried to make the food taste nice so it would make the patients feel better.

Our house on Sheridan Road was bought just before I was born. It had a big front porch with stone flower boxes, and two wide swings—a lovely place to sit on a summer evening. In the big hall inside, on one side was the coat room and the stairs; on the other was the front parlor, a room we rarely used, except for the pretty square piano where I practiced when I was taking piano lessons. Straight ahead was the big dining room with a door to the kitchen on one side and, on the other, a conservatory where my mother cared for all her plants.

Beyond that was the library, the room where everyone always went to sit and visit. One side was a wall of bookshelves protected by glass doors; when I was first learning to read, I used to walk along it and try to puzzle out the names of the books. Two sides had windows looking out into the garden with one huge, glass window that looked out over the garden to the lake.

Up above the library was an unheated room with windows all the way around, which we called the sleeping porch. When I was little, I kept all my toys there until the weather got too cold. And sometimes I slept there in cold weather under a pile of quilts. Beyond the windows, the night sky was deep blue, and you could hear the waves rolling up on the beach beyond the house next door and breaking at the seawall at the edge of the garden. And when it rained, the rain beat softly on the tin roof overhead, the sound joining the susurrus of the lake rolling toward the shore.

Because it was a big house, my mother always needed help. When I was very small, Mrs. Marozeck took care of me. I think her main job was doing all our family laundry. Even my dolls' dresses were washed and ironed, a thought that still astonishes me. Johanna Taibl and her sister, Anna Lukina, used to come to cook and serve when we had big parties. I remember one of them once showing me how you stretch dough out on a table to get the fine, thin texture you need to make strudel.

And most of all, there was Minnie Borgmann, who came to cook for us when I was about ten. Her cooking was marvelous. I remember my brother, then a widower who was cooking for four hungry teenagers, figure out how to make what we called "Minnie Potatoes," a kind of scalloped potato dish she did for us often. Not only were the meals wonderful, we got homemade bread and rolls, too. And when we had guests, she always remembered what each of them liked to eat. She was extraordinary.

She was also devout. After she retired, she moved to a Catholic nursing home in Wisconsin near her relatives. My husband and I used to stop and visit her there every so often.

Once one of the nuns told me Minnie used to go to the chapel and sit facing the altar.

"Are there some special prayers you say?" this nun once asked her.

"No," Minnie said. "I look at Him and He looks at me."

That is a sense of the divine presence that still awes me.

FAINTING
by Pat Lee

When I was very young, my family and I attended Sunday morning Mass at St. James Catholic Church on Bridge Street. We always sat three or four pews from the back, which meant a long trek to the altar if we were receiving Holy Communion. Although never late, we were also not likely to hibernate early in the more commodious but sparsely populated front or middle pews. We didn't rush in at the last minute, either. We dipped our fingers in the holy water font, made the sign of the cross, scouted a pew, genuflected, knelt for a quick prayer, then settled in and waited for the show to start.

I didn't think of it as a show in those days when going to church was almost like breathing. The church's interior had elongated lights suspended from the ceiling. The simple altar seemed pure and holy. The two side altars, one for Mary, the other for Joseph, held their large, benign statues. The communion rail started at one side of the church and flowed past these altars to the other. Red-carpeted steps led up to the rail.

From our seats, I had a hard time seeing everything going on up front but, since there was a daily eight o'clock Mass for children in all grades at St. James School, I knew exactly what was happening. Thus, my sister and I could concentrate on other things, like the fur coats on the large ladies in front of us. When we stood up, Marilyn and I would often reach forward and try to pet those coats, while being very careful not to disturb in any way the people inside them. At times, we gazed, mesmerized, by the fox fur scarves some ladies wore, the little fox heads' bright beady eyes staring back at us. If the Mass got drawn out or I got very warm, I simply fainted away. I don't know why. Daddy would carry me out. I had a vague suspicion that there was something wrong with me, but nobody was telling. We didn't discuss it later, and I hoped a repeat performance would not disrupt them too often.

One Saturday morning, as my Aunt Barbara and I were watching weddings in Polish St. Adalbert's Church, a huge cathedral-like bastion, I woke up to find myself being lugged out in my aunt's strong arms. Aunt Barbara loved weddings, and I'd accompany her to the nine o'clock one, stay for the ten o'clock Mass, waiting for the eleven o'clock bride to parade in. It was a three-bride morning. That day, we no doubt missed the entrance of the ten o'clock bride. Maybe all the color and costumes added to my growing need to survey the landscape of all things female, especially dresses: their color, cut, and fit. Certainly, when my friend Delores and I went to the movies, we'd talk almost incessantly about Alice Faye and what she wore, critically picking out details we knew were wrong for her. Experts at eight and nine, we were critical thinkers, annoying little girls, thankfully almost alone in the theater in the middle of an afternoon. My fainting spells did not occur in that venue.

As I've said, going to church was almost like breathing for me. As soon as I began school at age six, I was in church almost every day. At ages seven and eight, we made our first confession and communion. I'd often be there on Saturday afternoon going to confession. The priests sat in the middle portion of little houselike structures on each side of the church down from the side altars. There was a grate on either side by the priest's face that he could shoot open or close as one sinner after another vacated the space on either side. The grate's noise alerted me, with a slight leap of the heart, that my turn would be next.

What to say? What would the penance be? I had to figure out in numbers how often I swore or disobeyed my parents, how often I fought with my sister. I never thought of not going to confession. One did it in order to cleanse one's soul, make it pure again.

I worried more for my father than I did for me. I thought I was pretty holy, but I did not want Dad to go to Hell. I knew he was headed there unless he was lucky enough not to have committed a mortal sin. Mortal sins could be erased but left scars on the soul. Since he went to confession only about once a year, I could not be sure what lurked on the soft underbelly of his soul. In fact, confessing only once yearly may have equaled mortal sin in and of itself. The problem with mortal sin was that if you carried it and then pranced out in the street and got hit by a truck and died, you'd go to Hell. Not purgatory, no chance of Heaven. I was a true believer, a confessor, a pray-er, a rosary fiend, a missal advocate, a worried, anxious child. I thought too much. I worried too much.

There was much to see and hear and contemplate in church. Latin or not, I'd try to follow the Mass in my missal, an unattractive, unwieldy book whose only virtue to my mind was its thin, crinkly pages. I was a rosary nut. I had a dark red, faceted, beaded one. I loved that rosary and wish I had it today, not to pray on it, but to hold, look at, and feel the warmth of all those early memories. My sister and I made rosary bags, and our friends wanted them too, so we made bags for them. They were simple, drawstring receptacles, cut out of Mother's never-ending leftover fabrics. She sewed almost all of our clothes. We could cut any size bag we wanted, fold over its top, and sew a passage where sturdy ribbon could be woven through, thus pulling the thing closed.

My father's rosary had meaning for me too. He never used a prayer book, only his rosary. I loved it and wanted it when he died, but it was woven through his fingers as he lay in his casket and was buried with him. His rosary was made up of dark brown, oval beads, very smooth and shiny. It crumpled down into a little pile, unobtrusive in its own way but for its substantial cross, which let you know how important that pile of beads was.

My rosary was not so elegant. One day it sustained five go-arounds on the beads, prayers said very fast, just to see how many rosaries I could get in. Where did all those prayers go? Did I dedicate them to people I loved? Did I pray to finally stop swearing or biting my nails? Or quit the fainting spells? I do not know. One could say that mine was a simple little life, but it wasn't really, overblown as it was by a not-so-simple imagination. In those days you were usually alone with your thoughts. You didn't share these things. You just did what you were told and ravaged your mind on your own.

SCHNECKLE
by Helen Levy

"Schneckle, we're going to be having lots of houseguests staying with us in the next few months. You'll be sharing your room with some of them, so it's important that you put your toys away every day and pick up your clothes."

Those were my mother's words to me at the end of the year 1938. My parents had been the first of our family to flee Germany. During their courtship, when my father proposed marriage, my mother accepted only on the condition that they leave Germany as soon as they were married. She explained that she had dated an Austrian who showed her a map of Europe marked for the elimination of Jews.

Mother convinced Dad to seek work out of the country. With the help of family abroad, he managed to get job offers from South Africa and the United States. After some deliberation, they chose the United States, deciding that it was halfway between their two families, one in Germany and the other in Australia.

They married twice in February 1934, first in London so that mother could maintain her English citizenship in order to immigrate on English quotas, and then in Germany after my mother's conversion to Judaism in order to marry my father. They sailed for New York the next week from Hamburg with limited funds permitted by the German government.

As soon as they arrived in New York, they bought a second-hand car and began their trip to their new home in New Orleans, where Dad had his job. Mother insisted on stopping in Washington, DC, to see the capital of their adopted country. Seven flat tires later, they arrived in New Orleans and began to live the American Dream.

Dad had been educated as a textile engineer and worked at the family textile factory in Germany, the Julius Schmidt & Co, AG. Now he was a traveling salesman for a textile company, spending long, hard days on the road. While he drove around Louisiana selling clothing to small shops, Mother modeled the housedresses and outfits at each stop. The Louisiana drawl was a challenge and being away from family an adjustment, but they were in a friendly, safe environment.

I was born in New Orleans on the hottest day on record. I am told that I slept in a dresser drawer. My paternal grandparents were so anxious to meet me, their first grandchild, that they sailed to America from Stuttgart in 1936 for a brief visit.

Eventually my parents moved north and settled in Chicago where they began meeting others who had immigrated. We lived in a three-bedroom apartment on the third floor of a three-story building on Ingleside Avenue in Chicago's South Side.

The situation in Germany was growing more threatening. On November 9, 1938, my grandfather was arrested by the Nazis and interned in Dachau. He was given the option of being released from the concentration camp and allowed to flee if he signed over his home and business to the German government. He also negotiated visas and passage for thirty-seven relatives.

By the end of 1938, my parents were able to sign affidavits and sponsor family members who arrived on our doorstep, seeking a roof over their heads and comfort. That's when I was recruited to keep a clean room. There were grandparents, uncles, aunts, and cousins, totaling thirty-seven over a period of two years.

Fortunately, they all managed to find places to live and some sort of work to support themselves, and my parents were lucky that they could help all of them. Every member of our family who wanted to was able to emigrate.

Not long ago, I met one of the cousins, who told me that she had shared my bedroom with me for nine months. She had arrived at sixteen and had to finish a year of school living at one address. As her father was getting resettled, she lived with us. I was only four years old and didn't remember. All these years later, she told me that I was a good roommate and kept my room clean.

FIRST LOVE
by Enid Baron

The day my husband departed this Earth was the day I lost my sanity. I have to confess that I was ready to lose it. Living out the roles I had been assigned—wife, mother, daughter—was a high-wire act without a safety net, and I never knew when I was going to fall off and splinter into a million pieces.

One weekend in the nineteen seventies, my husband and I went on a retreat with a group of temple friends to a summer camp in Wisconsin, where several times a day we "unmasked" ourselves to each other as much as we dared. It was after completing what was called a trust exercise during which half of us were blindfolded and led around the room by the other half that our rabbi compared me to a fine porcelain bowl. I could have taken this as a compliment but instead, I realized he could see how fragile I was.

It was years later that I learned that this was both figuratively and literally true when I was diagnosed with Marfan Syndrome, a genetic mutation on the chromosome for fibrillin, which carries the gene for connective tissue. Unwittingly, I was a walking dry bones, my muscles and joints and tissues so loosely connected as to cause any number of problems: scoliosis, underdeveloped muscles, and the silent killer, an aortic aneurysm. Trying to return a volleyball over a net bent back my wrists with such force that I had to let other players take over for me. My schoolmates, who knew how inept I was in gym class, groaned when I wound up on their teams. Perhaps my mother knew it all along, always worrying about my falling, which I was prone to do throughout my childhood. Perhaps it was the reason that in later years, she was always on the lookout for a husband for me, someone who would pick up the pieces whenever my connective tissue or my nerves failed me.

I tried to escape at every opportunity from the world I inhabited, where my mother's thwarted ambition colored the fabric of our lives and my father's shame at his inability to make a better living did the same. While my older sister rebelled at every opportunity, I resorted to fairy tales, children's novels, movies, and daydreams. I dared not take up space in my parents' lives, which were troubled enough without having to deal with the problems of a fearful, insecure child who had to be urged to "go out and play." Because I was physically presentable, and a "nice" child, I was included in the other girls' birthday parties and in what is now referred to as junior high, the boy-girl parties which were de rigueur. I have a distinct memory of retreating to a sofa on a sunporch during a game of spin-the-bottle where I waited in a dream state for one of the boys I fancied to come and find me. Snow White's story had become my story by then, but when Prince Charming failed to materialize, I forced myself to return to the party.

By eighth grade, the boys I had grown up with had become mysterious creatures, their ears flattened against their heads like whorled seashells, the tender backs of their necks revealed after fresh haircuts, the way they argued and bellowed to each other and rode their bikes at breakneck speed, and how footballs and baseballs, any kind of ball, seemed to fit into their hands as if they'd been made for them. I loved hearing the sound of bat meeting ball followed by a wild scramble to get to first or second, sliding into the base without regard for bruises or sprains. How was it possible that in the face of broken ankles or torn ligaments, they could remain dry-eyed, even when they had to be half-carried off the playing field?

Boys were enigmas: soft and tough, cruel and tender, gentle and angry, quick-witted and witless. I would spot them slouching down the hall or riding the bus home from high school with their books pressed against their crotches, like shields. Whenever I got within five feet of one of my idols, my tongue stuck to the roof of my mouth and my mind went blank. Ordinary boys were no problem. Boys with pimples or funny-looking noses or sloping shoulders—those I could talk to, even flirt with. But it was the wild, handsome boys I adored, the ones who knew they could get any girl they wanted, boys who swaggered down the hall in their fraternity jackets and tight jeans, scuffing their penny loafers along the floor.

As if she'd been dropped from a Scandinavian fairy tale, Seva Gatewood showed up at school one day. She had corn-silk hair and eyes as blue as lakes and, when she walked into history class, the boys looked as if they'd been struck by lightning. She had one of those bodies that seemed to move as if it had a mind of its own, as if it had nothing to hide, unlike the rest of us who wore girdles that flattened our buttocks and bras that made our boobs stick out like armor. By the end of the period, the boys were climbing over each other trying to walk Seva to her next class while the girls whispered together in the back of the room. And even if the girls had had the decency to invite her to join them at lunch time, she would already have been mobbed by the football team who would have claimed her as their rightful trophy. It wasn't long before some girl spread the rumor that Seva had hooked up with the group of "fast" boys who reputedly used to drive up to Indiana where they could buy beer and hang out at someone's parents' summer cottage. "Nice" girls refused to speak to her and then one day she didn't come to school and we never saw her again. But I never forgot her and, although I knew I would never have the courage to live my life as fully as she, I kept her in the back of my mind as a symbol of the freedom I longed for.

I had a boyfriend by the end of high school, a freshman from the University of Chicago. He was tall and well built with lovely blue eyes and chestnut hair that curled at the nape of his neck. When he went home for the summer, he gave me a photo of himself and a pendant with a gold C on it for Chicago. I sobbed uncontrollably in the girls' bathroom the day he left. We corresponded all summer but, by the time he drove up to the University of Illinois where I was a freshman that fall, I had fallen in love with a senior whose blonde hair fell in a pompadour across his forehead. He wore a black aviator jacket and drove his own car and was in one of the slickest fraternities on campus. The boy from University of Chicago didn't stand a chance.

I would fall in love several times during college, but those were puppy love romances. The medical student who barged into my life when I transferred to the University of Chicago was the Adonis I'd always dreamed of, his body as perfect as the statues in Greece's museums—long, perfectly muscled legs, shoulders that were as broad as they were strong, eyes that could be steely or teasing, and a strong, stubborn chin. He had a quick temper, a ready wit, and a worldliness I had never encountered in any of the boys I had dated. When he stood at the kitchen sink in his dank basement apartment wearing nothing but a pair of khaki shorts, washing his socks, I wanted him more than I'd ever wanted anything in my life.

He used to bring me home to dinner at the Gold Coast apartment where his parents resided. There was a desk in the marble foyer manned by a uniformed attendant, a gentleman of the old order who guarded the residents' sanctity like a panther, only allowing expected visitors past the lobby door. Upstairs lay a world of Persian carpets, hushed lights, antique furnishings, and painted *santos* from cathedrals in New Mexico, where the family had a second home.

Naïve as I was, it had never occurred to me that, as a Catholic, he drew the line between "good" girls and "nice" girls, which was why he put off taking me to bed for a very long time. I loved him nevertheless and, when one day he gave me a key to his apartment, I took this to be a token of an unspoken commitment, as significant as a fraternity pin. Looking back, I believe that my having his key signified that I had lost his respect by having sex before marriage. Still, I continued to hope that in time he would love me again. When my period was late by several weeks, he never skipped a beat but began planning how we would quickly be married in the chapel at Holy Name Cathedral. That weekend, he tied an apron around my waist when I went into the kitchen to help his mother after dinner, a sign to her that our relationship should be taken seriously.

When my period eventually showed up, I considered not telling him at first, but realized that I could only fool him for a month or two, long enough to hold the wedding, and possibly even become pregnant. It was then I came face-to-face with the reality of the situation, my marrying in the Catholic church in a ceremony my parents would certainly not attend. There would be papers I would have to sign promising that I would raise our children Catholic. At parties, I would dread anti-Semitic jokes. It was an impossible situation, but still, I could not give him up and he would not break it off with me. The following summer, he and his roommate left for a motorcycle trip through Europe. Every day, I searched the mail for a postcard but when none arrived, I assumed that this was his way of breaking things off. It never occurred to me that he might remember how my mother had shunned him when he came to pick me up at home, and he might have been protecting me by not dropping me a postcard at my parents' home.

Toward the end of that summer, a boy I'd gone out with fixed me up with a friend of his. I pictured a tall, lanky fellow with a craggy face, à la Abraham Lincoln. But when I opened the door of my parents' apartment, I discovered a boy who was a couple of inches taller than I was, with a broad, Russian-Jewish face, whose name was Lew, short for Lewis. A Harvard Law School key dangled on a gold watch fob from his trouser pocket. When my mother asked him to wipe his feet on the mat at the front door and he did so without hesitating, I realized that here stood the man I was destined to marry, not the love of my life but the substance of my future.

FAMILY
MATTERS

PROBLEM SOLVING IS WHAT IT'S ALL ABOUT
by Ruth Sherman

Finally, Mama agreed to my taking the train alone to get to Bubbe Meyta's house in Brooklyn. I was the ripe age of thirteen and sort of street smart, so I did not anticipate any problems getting back to the Bronx as long as it was before dark. I made the trip to Brooklyn successfully and, in order to get back while it was still light out, I spent about forty-five minutes with Bubbe and took off.

Mama had given me detailed instructions on which train to take and where to get off. This would be close to where we lived in the Bronx. Also, I was to call Mama, and she would meet me at the station. Unfortunately, I dozed off, and when I awoke it was dark out, and I had gone way past my station. I saw that I was in a not-too-hot section of the Bronx, so I exited the train and walked down the steep flight of stairs to the street. At the bottom of the stairs was a "candy" store, which translated to a soda fountain, some stools, and a public pay phone.

Of course, by this time Mama had become frantic, and so had Bubbe Meyta. So when I called collect, Mama quickly accepted the charge. I then proceeded to tell her where I was.

"*Oy vey is Mir*" (Oh woe is me), she screamed. "Don't move. Papa and I are coming to getch you. Just stay in da kendy staw." So there I sat on the stool waiting. About ten minutes later, a squad car pulled up in front of the store and one of New York's finest entered

"Wherz da Porto Rican who's followin' ya? Yar Root Nelson, right?"

"How do you know my name? Are you really a cop, or what?"

"Goilie, ya tink yar Lana Toyna [Lana Turner]? Get in da cah. Ahm takin' ya home!"

When we pulled up in front of my building, all the neighbors were outside with Mama, who was sobbing hysterically. She immediately ran up to me and hugged me hard, muttering in my ear, "Shah, don't say nuttin'. Ya tink Papa end I vould go to dat *shvartz* (black) place? I called da puleece and told dem ya ver bein' followed by a Porto Rican fella. So it verked out hokay alda vay around."

MY MYTHIC CHILDHOOD
by Penelope Whiteside

As I grow older, I see in myself the same tendencies that marked the generations that preceded me. I look back on my childhood as a time of safety that no longer exists. I grew up in the nineteen fifties, in the country—Seymour, Connecticut, to be exact. Our town had a population of eight thousand, but most of us were spread out among the hills, which are studded with rocks and stonewalls and trees that had to be cleared regularly if even poor farmland was to be available.

Behind my family's house were four hundred acres of such land, owned by the farmers on either side. Mr. Mead and Mr. Jyckavitz pursued their livelihoods in very different fashions. Mr. J., who had worked in a coal mine for twenty years to save for his land, had a shiny new tractor and plows. Mr. Mead, whose family had owned his land since the seventeenth century, walked with a harrow behind his Clydesdale-sized horses, Tom and Jerry. My family had purchased four acres from Mr. Mead in 1940 and had remained cordial neighbors with him. Mr. J. and his wife were Polish and spoke little English.

In my memory's eye, there is a picture of a New England pasture at dusk. It is an image of emptiness, of November trees silvered by moonlight, of land that slopes downward toward a river two miles away. There are distant voices connected to this landscape. In January, my young parents and their laughing friends are sliding down the hill behind our house on flexible flyer sleds in the deepening moonlight. I am in my bed over the garage, not quite asleep, still waiting for the forlorn sound of the 9 p.m. train whose horn will echo across the far hills and valleys as it speeds in the night from NYC to Boston. As the train passes, I will turn over on my stomach so that the small hairs on my back can shiver at its sound.

The next afternoon, after the yellow school bus has deposited us at our gates, the boy and girl from across the street, and my brother and I, will try the sleds ourselves. The crust of snow that my parents aimed their skating sleds across has turned sticky in the bright winter sunlight. If we want to ride, we'll have to pack down a path, which we do, four abreast. Finally the path is ready. We flop on our stomachs, two to a sled, past Mr. Mead's pump house, abruptly turning toward the rickety shed with its rusty equipment, and then down the last hill straight into the barnyard, trying not to land in the large manure pile. We pull the sleds back up the hill and ride again and again, sitting, reversing positions of riders until the lowering sun causes us to turn to our separate homes.

Sunday is a time for visiting. I hear the agreeable crunch of gravel in our driveway. My grandfather has aimed his black Pontiac between the stone walls, rolling to a stop in front of the garage. My paternal grandparents live seven miles and a pleasant country drive away. Eventually they might get a cup of tea or a cocktail but neither is expected on these drop-in visits. My grandfather is a kind, just man with old man's halitosis. He perches me on his knee and sings late nineteenth-century ditties such as "She's got rings on her fingers, bells on her toes." My grandmother wears a dress with a matching hat. She is always smartly turned out. She sometimes tells me of her days as a schoolteacher in a one-room schoolhouse when she was sixteen, seventeen, eighteen. She used to go skating with her students on the nearby pond after reading, writing, and arithmetic. It was her job to start the schoolhouse woodstove before the students arrived. Her pupils would place their potatoes near the fire, which would cook them in time for lunch.

My grandmother married my grandfather at nineteen. He was quite a catch, having not one but two horses. Right now, she and my mother are discussing the latest parties, who wore what, and what was served, and talking mean about Mrs. Jerolman, a woman who always slaps her cards when she plays bridge. There is another crunch of gravel in the driveway. My aunt and uncle have also arrived for a visit. My uncle is president of a local bank. His face is deadpan unless he is laughing at his own jokes.

We spend long afternoons with my grandparents on the striped couch, with my aunt and uncle opposite my parents on the lumpy loveseats in front of the fireplace. The total lack of decorating sense is perfectly natural to me. The drapes on the three colonial windows present green-and-brown hunting scenes, which have no color correspondence with the intricate navy-and-orange pattern of the large Oriental rug or the smaller purple Persian rug that lies just beyond the living room arch in the hallway. The blue-and-gold striped armchair and the pink roses on the sofa add their liveliness. Only the love seats, encased in gold slipcovers, are plain.

Today, my uncle announces that Mr. Noble, a neighbor of his, will be driving his new Cadillac to Florida. Mr. Noble travels from Connecticut to Florida every winter, stopping several times along the way. I have heard this conversation before. Only the car is different. Mr. Noble's intended route is closely examined by the men. My father and grandfather weigh in with what they consider better routes to Florida, only to be countered by my uncle who, after all, is more intimate with Mr. Noble than either of them. As a child, I perched on the striped armchair, hoping for some tidbit, some peek into the adult world. Getting through Sunday afternoon is always a challenge, but even the boring ride of Mr. Noble is to be preferred to the long naps my parents take, leaving us kids to our own devices on the unavoidable slope toward Monday.

At supper time, standing on the green kitchen linoleum, my parents drink their Canadian Club as we kids dig into Chef Boyardee. The yellowish light of the ceiling fixture glares down upon us. From the pantry where the Bendix radio is kept come the welcome voices on the radio shows we all love. The evening turns a welcome corner. "Time for Beulah," "Our Miss Brooks," and "Jack Benny" have begun. When I am ten, we finally got a television set. "Milton Berle," "Sid Caesar," "Ed Sullivan," "The Firestone Hour," and "Lux Video Theater" will replace the old radio comedies, but these will be after-supper events.

On a bright June day in 1950, I see myself standing with my brother, Jim, and Peter and Wendy, the brother-sister pair from across the street. We are gathered at the end of our driveway waiting for the bus that travels the countryside picking us all up. Peter informs us that the Chinese have just invaded "Chosen." The Concord grape vines have begun their yearly climb on the stone wall. Bluebirds sing on the lawn. Where on Earth is Chosen?

Later, we will refer to Korea, not Chosen. War will come into our lives via the television news, as will the threat of nuclear attack. We will learn to crouch under our desks at school, and I will prepare a few bandages and canned goods for the place under the cellar stairs. My parents will shrug off the idea of nuclear attack, but I will remain worried. On this particular June day, though, I am just a fifth grader, waiting with my friends and brother as the yellow school bus labors up the hill, noisily changing gears. I take comfort in the fragrant grass where Mr. Mead's bull is now chained for grazing, and in the flight of the bluebirds.

OF BOOKS AND BICYCLES
by Dorothy Chaplik

Years after we were grown, my brother Mike and I developed an open, affectionate relationship. Although we lived in separate cities, in separate states, we visited several times each year, and kept in close touch by telephone or letter, no matter how far from home we roamed. But in our early days, there were no visible signs of friendship.

My earliest recollection begins when I was three years old and vaguely aware of a shadowy space between us. Before too many years went by, scorn and condescension drifted freely toward this small, female person who, unwittingly, had intruded on his princely role in the family. As we grew older, we communicated by exchanging slippery little slaps, barely skimming the surface of the other's shirt or sweater-sleeve. The first to be injured was quick to establish the inevitable chain of reciprocal slaps which went on, back and forth, until mother's patience grew thin and she cried out, "Stop it, both of you, this minute!" When we finally gave up this one habit that connected us, we also stopped speaking, except to remind each other, in acerbic terms, of the unfinished business of dishwashing that we shared on alternate days, to spare our working mother. Yet, two widely isolated incidents took place over the years that inspired hope for the future.

The first important event occurred when I was five, starting school and immersed in the world of alphabet images. As I learned to read, I pleaded with my mother for a library card, because *he* had one. He smirked at that, but when at last mother relented, my well-traveled, eight-year-old brother had the responsibility of escorting me to the library in our neighborhood. He was quick to remind me that I scarcely was ready for such serious activity. Shaking his finger at me, he said, "They'll punish you, if you ever tear a page. Or you leave pencil marks on a book. Or if you lose a book. They'll take your card away." I was properly cautioned and, side-by-side, we walked the few blocks toward our library on the northwest side of Chicago.

Mike balanced several books in the crook of his right arm. As we approached a busy avenue, he suddenly reached down with his free arm and grasped my hand, squeezing it tightly as he half-dragged me across the street. Just as suddenly, as I set both feet down on the sidewalk, he dropped my hand. For a brief moment, I felt his tender brotherliness, and remembered it forever.

Entry to my brother's world was closed during most of our high school years. Though we had similar literary interests, we never shared them. It seemed that the three-year gap between our ages progressively strengthened the notion of his superiority. Perhaps it was his defense as the only male sibling in a family with three sisters. Or it may have been an attitude supported by gender values of the times. Didn't my father once remind me that girls didn't need schooling? They would get married and be supported by their husbands.

Times changed and moved on, and after World War II was declared, Mike, at twenty-two, was drafted into the army. Though unhappy to interrupt his journalism studies, he was eager to become a soldier, dreaming perhaps of becoming a war hero. His farewell to a sorrowful mother and sisters contained a droll message: "Men go off to war; women stay home and cry."

After military training, he was sent to France; and not long afterward, a letter arrived, addressed to my younger sister and myself, and provided the second of those rare moments. Inside the envelope was a birthday check for ten dollars, with a brief note, as follows: "Buy used bicycle for the two of you to share. Love, Mike." It was a bittersweet gift, because Mike had never owned a bicycle, and because now he was in the midst of a terrible war and might never come home again.

The bicycle was given good use. Earlier, I had learned to ride on bikes belonging to friends, always envious of them, but now I owned half of one. It helped me to explore neighboring communities and, of course, to teach our little sister to ride. We practiced on the wide cement sidewalk in front of the convent near our apartment.

Mike came home after the war, but didn't stay long, moving to New Mexico, to complete his university studies among stunning mountain views and mild weather. By the time we were both married, he was back at the same university as a professor of English Literature. On our first visit to Albuquerque, my husband and I were warmly welcomed to the sand-swept adobe house where Mike recently had brought his new wife. We spent a glorious week together, driving through the mountains with Phoebe, their faithful, incomparable dog, and combing shops where we were introduced to American Indian-made rugs, black pottery, and jewelry. At one small shop, I was mesmerized by a handsome Apache basket woven in the shape of a classical Greek urn, just a wee bit askew. When the shop owner asked an affordable price for the basket, I did not hesitate to make the purchase. As we left the shop, the basket snugly under my arm, Mike was in a state of disbelief. "For months," he said, "I've been trying to bargain with that man for that very basket, and at a much higher price." Had I been as generous as my brother, I would have gifted him then and there with that lovely work of art. But, for whatever it says about my nature, the basket has occupied a place of honor in my living room ever since that day.

In the following years, my brother and I traveled together to many places, local and abroad, always with our mates, sometimes with our children. One year we drove to a theater in Philadelphia, where a play Mike had written, based on a story by Franz Kafka, "The Metamorphosis," was produced as an opera. Mike had not seen the score beforehand, and later realized, forlornly, that the composer had sacrificed the dialogue to suit his music, ignoring the integrity of the story. Even so, that night a group of Mike's friends insisted on honoring the occasion with a burst of champagne.

My brother and I remained dear friends until separated much too soon by Mike's death when he was fifty-one. Hardly a day has gone by in the past many years that I haven't vividly recalled some small happening we once shared. The later, brighter days endowed the earlier, uncertain ones with a humorous and rosy glow.

BRAIDS
by Deanne Thompson

For the past few years it's not unusual to see men with their hair in braids, but back in the nineteen forties, men would not be caught dead with braids in their hair. At this particular time, my dad was working nights, and he always caught the last bus in the evening to get there. Before going to work, right after dinner, he would stretch out on the sofa and catch a few winks and then jump up at the last minute, throw his cap and jacket on, and run out the door for the bus.

One night while he was asleep my mother and I took the front part of his hair and made about five braids and applied a little lipstick and penciled in eyebrows, and like clockwork, he jumped up, threw his jacket and cap on, ran out the door to catch the last bus.

On his ride to work, a couple times he lifted his hat to speak to someone and he kept getting strange looks and smiles. When he got to work he removed his cap and jacket. The other guys started laughing and said, "Hey Red, trying a new make-up?" He went to the washroom and looked in the mirror and felt like he wanted to shoot us. Then he saw the humor and laughed and cleaned his face and combed his hair out. Now he understood why he was getting the weird looks on the bus. The next morning we had to promise not to do that to him again. After that, before he left the house he'd always look in the mirror first.

MOTHER RUSSIA
by Ruth Granick

A friend and I just saw the opera *Nixon in China*. Well, I saw two-thirds of it but walked out during the second intermission. The work was just too upsetting.

I was born in 1930, at the time when unions were constantly in the news—unions and employers. There were strikes, there were company unions, unions in name only. There were lockouts, sit-ins, picket lines, and scabs. My Uncle Harry was an ardent Communist, as were many among the artists and more politically aware. He was a writer. As a convert his faith was total, and anyone casting aspersions on his newfound belief was straight from hell and should be sent back. I don't know why my Uncle Al went the opposite way. My two uncles had frequent arguments, really nasty arguments. Finally Harry quit coming to family gatherings, while Al did attend. Al was, or seemed to me to be, a warm, kindly gent, while Harry was a porcupine with quills extending in all directions. Anyone near him would get hurt.

My Aunt Rosie termed herself a Communist. Her red activities consisted of a subscription to the *Daily Worker*, which I don't think she read, and an impractical attitude toward any cleaning woman she hired. They had to clean for a living, therefore they were poor and oppressed, and therefore they needed verbal assurance, kindness, and generosity. She chatted with them, they chatted with her, they got overpaid and left. The apartment was almost as messy as it was before they came.

At that time I was growing up with a mother who worked full-time, my father having fled when I was two years old. I was nine or ten years old, and we shared an apartment with an aunt and uncle for fiscal practicality. These people had no children, had no idea what a child was, what a child needed, except that a child should set the table and dry the dishes. I was alone most of the time. My mother sensed my loneliness and my vulnerability, and as I grew older she worried about me. Before sending me off to camp, she related to me the story of her abortion. Give yourself to a man, she warned, and see what results!

Unlike the USSR, which allowed abortion in its constitution, for the average American, abortion was illegal. It had to be done in secrecy without anesthesia.

"Come in, strip, lie down. Don't scream. OK, get up, get dressed, go home, and I never want to see you again." This account terrified me and made the USSR, with its marvelous constitution, seem like paradise.

About that time, I saw a film about World War II starring Dana Andrews. He was an American soldier in Europe. A whistling Russian boy walked ahead of him through the forest, guiding him toward the Nazi hideout. His whistles conveyed his information. Dana was handsome, the boy was Russian, the woods were beautiful. Russian folk music touched my soul, Russian ballet was unsurpassed, Russian novels felt like home. These were My People.

We moved. I was sixteen years old and now we lived with Mac and Rose. My Aunt Rosie was the one who took the *Daily Worker* and she knew something about Communism. This was at the time of the purge trials. Of course we did not believe in them, could not believe that Russians were tortured by other Russians into making false confessions. But suddenly our small family group started having its own kangaroo trials. I must have been a difficult teenager, and my aunt had no idea how to handle me. After dinner, we were called into the living room, my mother and I. I was told to sit down. My Uncle Mac, as chief inquisitor, was up to the job. He asked me whether I had done this, or had said that. Evidently he and Rosie had conferred. I don't remember whether I tried to save myself by lying or whether I confessed. Then he asked why I had done this or that, then he asked how I felt about doing this or that. By that time I was in tears, totally humiliated. My mother, who felt beholden to the relatives who took us in, although she paid her share of rent, food, and utilities, sat silent, horrified by this narrative of my bad behavior. There was no punishment after the trial, the trial was traumatic enough, and I was told to mend my ways.

I still loved the USSR, its culture, its language, which my grandparents spoke. But something about it was not quite right. Stories about pogroms, about raids, with rapes, murders, thefts perpetrated by Russians upon the Jews, whom Russians did not consider Russian, reached us. These stories reflected my understanding of my world. Russians didn't want us, my father, aunts, and uncles did not want me.

Nixon in China. There was a ballet, a danced narrative, which was quite beautifully done. There was uniformity in the chorus outfits and mien as, I was learning, there was uniformity in Communist countries. There was a spoken regard for the People, at the same time that the People were treated with callousness, with cruelty. I usually listen to operas. I do watch them, but the music is most important to me. I'm sure there was music in this opera. My friend spoke of it, but to me it was Mother Russia rejecting us all. It was cruel, it was heartless, and I could not stay 'til the end.

MY AUNT MARGARET PLAYED THE PIANO
by Sarah Mirkin

My Aunt Margaret played the piano. In fact, she played it very well. I became aware of this the summer I was five. We were staying with my grandparents because my father was in the process of changing jobs. My Aunt Margaret stayed there too. Her husband had been killed in the Battle of Tarawa in the Pacific in 1944, and she had come home to live with her parents for a while. I remember the small banner that hung in the window of the house designating a family with someone in the Armed Forces. It had a red border, a white inner background, and it hung on a gold cord. The blue star in the center indicated that someone in the household was in the service. That summer we stayed in my grandparents' house, that blue star had been replaced with a gold star.

My aunt practiced on a piano that was set in a room off of the main living room, a music room where one could concentrate without being interrupted. If I wasn't at the beach or searching for frogs in the ravine at the end of the street, I would listen to her practice. I would sit outside the music room, out of sight, and listen to small sections being played over and over again, then linked to larger sections which were played over and over again. I was very aware of repetition; that was the beauty of it. The repetition only stopped when the section had been played without error at least three times. She never acknowledged my presence. I actually believed that she didn't know 1 was there. I didn't want to share my experience of the sound with anyone. I wanted it to be mine.

One day she stopped in the middle of a phrase and called out, "Sally, come in here. I want to show you something." I had been discovered. But she wasn't at all annoyed by my presence. She had probably known all along that I was there. She put me on the piano bench next to her. Up on the music stand above the keyboard was a book with lines and dots on it. Some of the dots were filled in and some were only an outline. She explained that the five lines in front of me held those dots at various levels and that was how you knew what key to play on the piano. She said the lines were called a "staff," and the black dots were called "notes." She showed me black dots that lay on top of lines, or between lines, or under lines, or right smack in the middle of lines.

She laid my small hand on the keyboard, with my right thumb on what she said was middle C. She told me to keep my thumb there and asked me to look at the staff, and she pointed to a note. "That note," she said, "is middle C on the page. And the key your thumb is on is middle C on the keyboard. All you have to do is to look at the notes, one after another, and tell your fingers to play the notes you see on the keyboard you touch. I hit middle C. Zing! There it was. The staff and the eye, the hand and the key. That was how she could make all those magical sounds. She was seeing them on the staff, and I began the journey into the language of music.

In addition to the loss of her husband, my aunt suffered a number of other blows in her long life. At the age of ten she contracted rheumatic fever, which stunted her growth. She remained under 5 feet tall and never weighed more than 100 pounds. She remarried shortly after the war and bore two children, a boy then a girl. As an adult, the boy married badly to a woman who belittled him. His wife had a cruel streak. He buried his rage deep inside and died at forty-two of stomach cancer. The wife did not like my aunt, her mother-in-law, and took her children far away where my aunt never saw them. Aunt Margaret had a battle with breast cancer, lost her second husband to heart disease, and went to live near her remaining child. She continued to play the piano, to give lessons, and to play the organ for church services until she lost her sight three years ago. She can still hear, and she can still walk. She often makes her way to the keyboard where she plays what she can remember. Her letters to me are of a steady hand. She always praises me, talks about her life without bitterness, and raves about her grandchildren. She is ninety-five.

As I developed my knowledge of the language of music and the skills of making that transfer from the notes on the page to the keys on the keyboard, the routine of practice built in me a fortitude that my aunt helped to develop. She never gave up until a passage sounded right and then she had to keep at it, or the skill would deteriorate. I see that discipline in her life. I try to imitate it in my life. She battled continual pain and loss with the fortitude of continual effort to make something beautiful.

MY INHERITANCE
by Ruth Sherman

My grandma was very poor, actually dirt poor. Every Sunday her son, my father, would go to visit her in her tiny furnished room in Coney Island. Coney Island was also dirt poor. You've got the picture. He would always stop on the way and get her some day-old bread and week-old oranges, and as a treat to himself for being a good son, he would stop at a strip show on the way home.

When Grandma was found dead in her furnished room, he felt apologetic that she had nothing left to give me. The only thing of any worth was her newly purchased false teeth. He carefully wrapped them and brought them home to me. My family was kind of "different," so I carefully accepted the gift and thought about what to do in proper reverence.

My friends and I were going up to a farm in upper New York State, and so I took the teeth with me knowing that I would find a proper burial spot. We invited some fellas back to our room at the farm and before we went out dancing, I put the teeth in a glass of water on the night stand. One of the guys, the big fat one, spotted the teeth and then started looking carefully in our mouths, but we all had our teeth. He called his pals into the bathroom and, after a hurried consultation, they left.

AUNT ALICE
by Deanne Thompson

I thought of many of my relatives over the years, and I remember many of them fondly and some not so fondly. But one I will always remember is my Aunt Alice. She was my father's older sister, but she had pushed her age back so many times she ended up younger than him when she died.

I won't say she was sweet, but she was kind and generous to a fault. All the children in the neighborhood were crazy about her, but most adults in her life just tolerated her. Probably because for someone who never had children she thought she was an authority on raising them. You could always hear her saying, "Parents just don't raise their children right," or "Parents don't teach their children manners," but children were always welcome to come over and visit her.

Her husband was a very quiet man who always agreed with anything she said. She would make a statement and say, "Ain't that right, Nel?" And he would always say, "Uh huh, uh huh." I only heard them argue once. He had disagreed about something she said, and she told him, "Shut up you old fool. You don't know nothing." He replied, "No, you shut up. You don't know nothing about anything." I was so shocked that I just sat there with my mouth open and then I had to giggle. She was embarrassed and said, "He's just testy today."

My dad had a quick temper. Aunt Alice could anger him before he even sat down, on his visits to her house, and he'd end up just leaving. Once I was visiting her and she made a remark that angered me so much that I didn't speak or go near her for eight years. It was a long time to not speak to someone, but I had just had enough of her opinions and sarcasm. Eventually we made up and she was very sweet and kept her opinions to herself.

My children mostly remember her dog, Adam. He wore eyeglasses, and it was a funny sight to see this little skinny dog coming down the street wearing eyeglasses. Aunt Alice died a few years ago, and I still miss her.

WHAT'S FOR LUNCH
by Diane Ciral

It's October 1956. Eisenhower is in the White House, Elvis Presley and Johnny Cash are playing on the radio, Ed Sullivan is on the TV, Mickey Mantle of the New York Yankees leads in home runs batted in and runs scored. And I am newly married without a clue on how to cook. Not only am I supposed to make breakfast and dinner but, since Shev works in a lumberyard on Goose Island where there are no nearby restaurants, I am supposed to pack a wholesome lunch for him every day.

There are just no cookbooks for lunch. I know about peanut butter and jelly sandwiches and ham-and-cheese sandwiches, but what goes into tuna fish salad or egg salad is beyond me.

I get along OK for a few weeks, but I know I need to do better. Three weeks of peanut butter and jelly, salami, and ham-and-cheese are beginning to wear a bit thin. Shev doesn't complain, but I know deep down that he isn't exactly enjoying his noontime meal.

At the checkout counter in the supermarket, I spy a magazine called "Family Circle" with the words "Creative Lunchbox Menus." I buy the magazine and quickly run down the store aisles gathering up all the magical ingredients necessary to make these gourmet lunches. I rush home with renewed hope. The first day's lunch is a baked bean, peanut butter, and bacon sandwich on Wonder Bread. No comment from my husband. Subsequent lunches are banana, tomato, and mashed sardines. Still no comment. When I finally get the courage to ask how he likes his lunches, he asks me to please go back to salami and ham-and-cheese, which I am happy to do.

Sometimes I give him leftovers from our dinner or hot dogs, which he can boil on a hot plate at the office, or hard-boiled eggs. I was sure I had given him cooked eggs in his lunch box one day, but evidently I had been in too much of a rush and forgot to cook them.

The result was the yolk and white running all over the papers on his desk.

One day I receive an unusual package in the mail. It is wrapped in brown paper, addressed to me. When I open it, I find a small wooden box with the letters "RIP." I open the box. There, resting inside, is a green, ossified hot dog. In my haste, I had reached into the freezer to get the hot dog, but I guess it must have been in there for a lot longer than I thought.

After fifty-two years, I continue to make Shev's lunches. I gave it up for a few months, telling him that he could phone in his orders with the rest of his staff or go to a nearby restaurant. One afternoon he tells me quite casually that his lunches consist of mostly deep-fried food or barbecued pork or tacos. I get the message and now I am back to the old routine. If *he* isn't retired at eighty-five, I guess I can't retire either.

THE WAR YEARS IN CHUNKING

by Stella Mah

Chunking was a sleepy river city in the early 1930s. I believe its importance developed because it is situated at the navigable head of the Yangtze River, which cuts a big gash from west to east across the middle of China and was the main conduit of travel from the interior to the city on the coast, Shanghai. I do not know the population of Chunking then, but it was nothing compared with Shanghai.

The government of Chiang Kai-Shek decided in 1936 to move the capital to Chunking from Peking before the Japanese invaded. The population did grow substantially. The city was on the north bank and had paved roads, electricity, and water and sewer services. But people like my family, who moved there during the war, lived outside the city, fearing the frequent bombing.

My father's company provided us living quarters on the south bank halfway up a steep hill. Because Dad was the boss, he was allotted a house in the center of the courtyard. I believe there were about four to six families plus a bunch of single employees.

Electricity was installed after a year or so but until we left in 1945, we never had running water or sewers. Roads were primitive, with one main road at the bottom of the hill. Access from the road to our home was by a series of steep stone steps. The sides of the hills rose in jagged peaks and became mountains with caves, which we used as bomb shelters during air raids. I remember well the nights when sirens rang out and my parents would race to the caves, my dad clutching my brother, and Mom hugging me in her arms, trying to calm my fears.

My father had an office in our compound for a little while but later moved to an office across the river in the city. Every morning, two men who'd been hired to carry water and waste, and as sedan chair porters, would carry Dad down the hill to the docks where he took a ferry across the river to his office. The process would be reversed in the evening. During the day, the porters carried water up from the bottom of the hill. This was stored in big earthen barrels. The men would also carry my brother and me to and from school three times a day, mornings and back and forth during lunch time. We would walk home at the end of the day because the porters would have gone to wait for Dad at the dock.

At the time, I thought nothing of the porters. I realized how hard their jobs were after I became an adult. They carried the water in two large buckets, one at each end of a bamboo pole across their shoulders. If they spilled too much water, it would mean additional trips. Carrying a sedan chair took two men, one in front and one in back. The seat for the passenger was in the middle. When they went up or down the hill, the man in the down position carried the most weight. My brother, always full of hijinks, would deliberately bounce up and down to see if he could make the men slip or fall.

The hill on which we lived was quite steep and was paved with jagged stone steps, which were not always properly aligned. One Sunday, my brother and I were playing a game and were running up and down around the house. It had rained the night before and the steps were wet. My brother, who was always in the lead, ran up some steps, slipped, and gashed his eyebrows. Blood poured down his face. Dad and Mom managed to stop the bleeding and took him across the river in a rowboat—the ferry did not run on Sundays—to get him to a doctor. The river is wide and quite rapid at Chunking, the water rushing from the Himalayas. Boulders dotted the river, creating rapids and hazards for boaters. The motorized ferry ride across took about twenty minutes. To cross in a manual boat was a dangerous affair and took about twice as long.

To this day, my brother has a scar that cuts his eyebrow in two.

In 2003, I had my first opportunity to visit Chunking after all these years. I wanted to see how it looked and whether my memory of it was accurate. I wanted to see the ferry dock, the south bank where we lived, and perhaps even the area where my school was. To my great disappointment, I saw none of these. When I voiced my disappointment to my father-in-law, he said, "You would not have recognized those places because the city has been completely rebuilt and developed."

Recently, I saw a picture of the dock area with a long, wide flight of steep stone steps. I have a vague memory of that. Chunking is now the most populous city in China, overtaking Shanghai. Chunking is now spelled Chongching.

THE HABERDASHER WHO SAVED THE FAMILY
by Helen Levy

On a sunny morning on August 6, 1879, sixteen-year-old Joseph Levi boarded the SS Gellert in Hamburg, Germany, to sail cabin class on his own to America. He left the small village of Freudenthal to avoid conscription in the German army. His documents state that he was a merchant, though his boyhood ambition was to be an artist or silversmith.

He started out as an apprentice in a clothing store in Cincinnati, Ohio. From there he moved to Peru, Indiana and later to Duluth, Minnesota. In 1892, he arrived in Muncie, Indiana, where he worked for the clothing merchant Charles Winter, and later for A.R. Wolff. In 1901 he purchased the New York Hat Company from the Friedlander brothers, who specialized in exclusive men's wear.

Uncle Joe was a dapper gentleman who wore boutonnieres in his lapel and smart stickpins in his ties. Charming with the ladies, he was in great demand at dinners and social events, and his judgment was greatly respected in civic affairs. He returned frequently to Europe to visit his parents and travel the continent. In 1931, the *Muncie Morning Star* reported that he had made ten trips abroad.

By May 1928, my father, who was then twenty years old, sailed to the United States to visit textile companies and learn about machinery and business practices for the family factory in Stuttgart. During his six months in the states, he established a good relationship with Uncle Joe. Later, this friendship proved to be extremely helpful.

By the 1930s, business travel outside of Germany was monitored, and life became difficult for the Levis and their Jewish compatriots. With the bad came some good, though, when my father met and fell in love with beautiful Elsa Kienzle, who was not Jewish. Their courtship was fraught with decisions about leaving home and where to relocate. They were married in February 1934, and left Germany immediately for a new life in the States.

My father found a job in New Orleans, where they made their first home. Eight months later, my mother gave birth to a baby girl who they named Helen-Joan. A year later, in September 1936, the Levi grandparents sailed to the United States to meet their first grandchild.

When Uncle Joe's health began to fail, my parents and I moved to Muncie to be with him and help him manage his company. In the fall of 1937, Uncle Joe died peacefully in his apartment at the Delaware Hotel with the three of us at his bedside. He was seventy-four. In his will he left bequests for his synagogue and favorite charities. More important, the will stipulated that, upon his death, each of his eight siblings or their issue living in Germany would receive their inheritance only if they appeared in person in the United States. Uncle Joe knew that if the money had been sent to Germany, his heirs would not have been allowed to leave the country. These bequests enabled the Levi kin to immigrate to America in 1939 and saved them from the Holocaust.

SAILING WITH BERNARD
by Sarah Mirkin

In the early days of our courtship, Bernard visited me at the family's summer home on Swan's Island off the coast of Maine. Even though we both lived in Minnesota, Maine was not alien to him. He and his family also owned a place on Long Pond, a pristine freshwater lake set in the middle of Mount Desert Island. In fact, to get to Swan's Island, one has to drive to the southern tip of Mount Desert to catch the state ferry out to the island. Because Long Pond is a freshwater lake, Bernard's boating experience had remained with the kind of vessels one uses on a small lake: canoes, row boats, small skiffs, kayaks. Although Mount Desert Island is itself surrounded by the Atlantic Ocean, it is a very large island. One can vacation there without being aware of the ocean. A causeway connects it to the mainland, so it doesn't seem off shore.

Swan's Island is an outer island in Penobscot Bay, a jutting of granite from the ragged sea shelf that creates all those islands along the famous coast of Maine. Swan's Island's only freshwater ponds are the quarry pond, from the days of granite quarrying at the end of the nineteenth century, and a large lily pond in the middle of the island. One cannot be anywhere on Swan's without being aware of the ocean. If one resides on Swan's Island year round, one probably makes a living as a lobsterman. Lobstering requires working out in the open Atlantic or in coves and harbors where the lobsters migrate. The work is hard and dangerous, requiring a lot of skill in understanding the treachery of ocean going in small craft. Boating is not recreational for the Swan's Island natives.

As the summer people began to come to Swan's Island beginning in the 1950s, they did not take up lobstering. It's not a vacation activity. However, many summer people were skillful boaters from other parts of the Atlantic coast who wanted a greater sailing challenge. Even these skilled sailors approach sailing off Swan's Island with caution, mooring their boats in the deep-set Burnt Coat Harbor and carefully rowing their dinghies ashore to a safe dock where they can tie up. Rowboats, small sailboats, small motorboats, and kayaks are used close to shore and in the several well-protected harbors of the island. Summer people, with or without boating skills, take lessons from the lobstermen and treat the ocean deep with great respect.

More than thirty years ago, Bob Solotaroff, my first husband, and I had acquired a Rhodes 19 to sail off the shores of Swan's Island. The Rhodes is a nineteen-foot day sailer, which has a sturdy keel and hull and can withstand strong winds, shifts in the current, and powerful tides. When Bob and I divorced, the Rhodes 19 was one of the luxuries I allowed myself to keep, and I loved that boat. My sailing skill was at its height at the time of Bernard's visit some years later, and I took him sailing several times. He was quiet, which usually meant that he was watching and making judgments. He asked no questions, but then the scenery was dazzling, the winds often brisk. It wasn't a time for questioning.

That winter it became necessary to sell the boat: two children in college, one income, and dwindling savings. I couldn't afford the Rhodes 19. My sailing skills declined. Bernard and I married shortly after that and moved to Chicago. Our lives became extremely complex with two sets of children, new jobs, and a new city. The love of sailing the Maine waters receded into the background. We continued to go each summer to Swan's Island. We were absorbed in building a new house on a special piece of land we had acquired. Building a modern home was one of Bernard's dreams, and he was immersed in the many decisions that go into building a new home, not to mention building it on a rather remote island.

I don't clearly recall his first mention of a boat, but I know that we had finished the house and were furnishing it. He came home one Saturday afternoon to tell me that he had found a used Rhodes 19 for sale, and he was going buy it for me. Two middle-aged lawyers, who sailed as a hobby, wanted to upgrade from their Rhodes 19 to a larger cruising vessel and were willing to sell the 1976 Rhodes for a reduced price. Bernard drove me to a boatyard on the northwest side of Chicago to look the boat over. There was another sturdy Rhodes 19 in its later years but immaculately maintained and dripping with equipment for a much larger boat. The lawyers had put as many playthings on the Rhodes as they could. They were ready to move on.

It was a loving gesture from Bernard, and I was thrilled. I hadn't sailed for several years, so I took some classes at one of yacht clubs in Chicago. I could still do it! Bernard had not said much about his role in this, other than as purchaser. At some point after that purchase, before we took the boat to Maine, he told me that several years ago he had taken an intensive sailing course on Lake Superior with some friends. The boat he had learned on was much larger than the Rhodes 19 and required much more sophisticated handling. I was looking forward to merging our two sets of skills on the Atlantic.

First we had to get a Rhodes 19 from Chicago to the coast of Maine, and we weren't going to sail it. Since the boat came with a trailer, we decided to pull it to Maine, a journey of 1300 miles. At that time we were busy acquiring things to furnish the new house. Why not use the boat as a U-Haul? So, on the eve of our usual summer departure for Maine, we loaded the cabin of the boat up with belongings. The trip took three days. We would proudly pull into the driveway of a friend somewhere along the way, stay the night, and show off our boat. We arrived on the island with our new old boat, parked it in the driveway, and unloaded the household goods. We then found a lobsterman to help us launch the boat, and motored it over to our new mooring. We rowed our dinghy back to the float and sat looking at that boat in the afternoon sun. It was beautiful, and we were going to enjoy it together.

The trouble began immediately. I was used to being captain of my boat and Bernard was used to being captain of everything else. I lacked the mechanical skills that the motor and the roller-reefing device demanded. But I had a natural sense for the feel of sailing the boat and had refined that skill over the years of owning the first Rhodes 19. I don't know what Bernard had learned in that course he took, but it didn't stick. Bernard could never remember from season to season that one pushes the tiller in the opposite direction from which one wants it to go. He would insist on taking the tiller, I would cast off, he would work the tiller in the wrong direction, and the boat would begin moving slowly but inexorably, not out of the harbor, but toward the rock ledge on the other side. There would be a moment of panic as I scrambled down from the bow of the boat to grab the tiller and turn the boat away from the rocks. He would be yelling to get out of the way, and I would be yelling to get out of the way. He would see the ledge approaching and would give control of the boat over to me. Even as I write this, my stomach is turning. The wind in the harbor is very unreliable because of the curve of the land on either side, so there are gusts of wind that puff at you and then disappear. If he were sailing, Bernard would overreact to those gusts, turning the boat into the wind, which brought it to a halt and left it prey to the next gust. And we would lose our momentum to get out of the harbor.

Studying the nautical chart, we would decide on a destination for an afternoon sail, or a route we would take. On that we could agree. Once in the boat one of us would hold the chart, pointing out depths, ledges, and sea-going markers, while the other sailed. That was how it was supposed to work once we got into the Rhodes.

However, getting onto the boat involved yet more problems. We needed to get to the Rhodes by rowing the dinghy. I could not get him to agree to kneel down, either in getting in or out of a boat, to put his hands on the gunnels (edges) of the boat right and left, and then, balancing his weight, to lower himself into the boat. He insisted on stepping into the boat. This is precarious for the person, his companion, and the boat, which, if overturned, could sink. He would step into the dinghy, feel the instability, be unable to release the foot still on shore, and would remain there straddling the two worlds. He did fall into the water once getting from the float into the dinghy. He looked pretty shocked. That water is extremely cold, so that cut our afternoon sailing short.

The waters we sailed are loaded with lobster traps, their location on the ocean floor indicated by brightly painted lobster buoys that are the signs of the owner of the trap. These buoys are to be avoided by all means: One, because the lobstermen use those buoys to identify the location of their traps, and two, because getting the rudder or the motor caught on the trap line brought the boat to a halt. Then it was up to the one not sailing to hang over the side of the boat with a boat hook and try to release the line from whatever it was caught on. Bernard either didn't believe that there were traps down there, or he was uneasy enough on the water to pay no attention to the buoys and to sail proudly on. I would sit up front using a boat hook to do my best to push the buoys away from us as he headed directly forward. If I had the tiller, I would tack back and forth to avoid the traps, and he would tell me to stop weaving; it was making him seasick.

Mostly there was a lot of arguing. We would invite good friends out for a sail where they would be treated to our incessant bickering. After several uncomfortable sails, they would politely decline another offer. We maintained several friendships by not inviting people to go sailing with us. In spite of all the conflict and confusion, the solidity of the Rhodes 19 kept us from capsizing. Like a well-trained dog, it knew how to right itself, even if the master was losing his way.

Bernard's antics in launching the boat at the beginning of the season and hauling it out of the water at the end of season became legendary on the island. To launch the boat, one carefully studies the timing of a high tide, pulls the boat to the launching area aside the ferry dock about an hour before high tide, and backs the boat into the water while it is still on its trailer. Then, as the tide comes in, the water lifts the boat off the trailer, the sailor uses the tiller to set the boat, now afloat, on its proper course, and he motors away from the launching area. As with the tiller, Bernard had it backwards. He would insist on bringing the boat to the water's edge just as the tide was cresting, back it into the water, and then sit in the boat watching the tide recede, as he and the boat got further and further away from the water. My hunch is that he did this on purpose, because he liked to see the islanders gather on the shore to watch the ground area widen between the boat and the shoreline, while Bernard sat in his Rhodes 19 reading his *New York Times*. This confirmed every prejudice the island fishermen had about summer people and their abilities on the water. Bernard probably had figured out after several years of sailing around Swan's Island that he wasn't going to be the sailor he wanted to be, so he might as well be the island clown.

Over the years, we managed to maintain our friendships by sailing only by ourselves, and we developed a raw kind of cooperation. We had our own chores as we prepared the boat for sailing, his more on the mechanical side and mine more on the sailing side. We would quietly comment to each other about the conditions of the day, I would take the tiller, and off we would go.

It's a strange thing about men. If they don't have full control, they lose interest and become careless and indifferent to the task at hand. Had I been more of a grown-up I could have gently instructed Bernard by manner of suggestion, not command, and perhaps he could have taken on a stronger role in our sailing enterprise. One looks back at so many situations with a "What if . . .?"

In mid-August of 2007, Bernard and I went sailing for what would be our last sail together. We were working at working together, and it was working. We each knew our own chores. The breeze was mild, so the maneuvering in the water was easy. At the end of each sail, we had developed a pattern of approaching the mooring where he would start the motor, I would haul the sails down, and we would move slowly toward the mooring flag. I would grab onto it, pull the mooring line into the bow-chock, tie it off, and we would come to a stop. That day, after a skillful conclusion to our sail, we rowed back to the float. As he climbed out of the dinghy, he said, "Well, we did that one pretty well, didn't we?" He died two days later.

Bernard was always seeking to improve whatever he was doing, to keep answering questions, to keep investigating a process until he was satisfied with how he was handling it. The many quirks in his character often pulled him off course, but he would pull himself back into line and journey on. His death interrupted his various unfinished journeys.

ANYTHING FOR THE KINDER (CHILDREN)

by Ruth Sherman

My uncle Al, who was known as Abbish, was my mother's youngest brother. He always lived with his parents and, when Zayde died, he stayed on with Bubbe Meyta. No, he was not gay, just "devoted," or whatever.

Many years later, when I was already married and had kids, my husband and I went to visit him in Miami Beach. He had retired there when he was forty and was living with a lady named Maureen. They were both dancers and would spend their nights whirling around under the stars in a Miami band shell.

While we were visiting, he started to reminisce about the old days and how he remembered their emigrating from Russia to Ellis Island. I said, "That must have been so terrible for you because didn't they put the immigrants in steerage at that time? Do you remember that, Abbish?"

"Oh, of course, but Bubbe Meyta, your Mama Rose, and I always had dinner at the captain's table."

I was amazed and asked him how or why that had been possible. "Well," says Abbish, "it was because Bubbe Meyta was sleeping with the captain."

A mother's sacrifice is never too great.

HARD TIMES

GROWING UP
THE HARD WAY
by Ruth Sherman

I was born in New York City seventy-five years ago but have spent the last fifty-five years of my life in Chicago. Specifically, I grew up in the Bronx, which was the essence of New York Jewry. My parents were quite bizarre but how was I to know that they were any different than any upper-lower-class Jewish family? Didn't every Jewish father take an enema every night after dinner? Didn't every other Jewish mother bite and pinch her only child?

When I entered the real world was when I started school and went into other homes and observed how different other parents were from mine. A *potch in tuchus* (pat on the rear) was the usual punishment, and I yearned for that. That was how a momma really showed love. Instead in my house there was a dance of abuse. Papa hit Momma who hit Ruthie.

As I entered puberty around the age of twelve, I made two life-altering decisions. One, that I would sleep with a knife under my pillow so that if Papa came near me, I would stab him. He knew about it, and it was sufficiently off-putting to him. The second one was that I would leave home as soon as I could earn a living and support myself. The physical and verbal abuses were intolerable, and I was getting out.

No one was allowed into our apartment. If there was a knock at the door, we had to lie down on the floor and not utter a sound. There was overwhelming clutter wherever you looked and it was impossible to find anything. If you needed something, you first had to inform my mother and she would scurry around, tossing things in the air, until she found what was requested. She would start screaming and insist on supervising any activity in the apartment. I was not even allowed to walk into the kitchen to get a drink of water from the encrusted faucet. She would fill a filthy glass and hand it to me, and I had to immediately give it back after I drank from it.

Momma would forage through the clothes piled on chairs and thus I would be given something to wear to school. Most of the time, if not all the time, the clothing was cast-offs from a cousin I had never met who was seven inches taller and twenty pounds heavier than I was. My mother would "alter" these clothes in a very primitive way, making huge flaps wherever they didn't fit. It was the underwear that did me in. The bloomers were huge, so they would get pinned with a very large safety pin, and I lived in fear that the pin would open and these hideous bloomers would fall to the ground and everyone would see.

I was very skinny and pale and wore large glasses. What a mark I was for kids to mock. Such pain! Did it make any difference that my intellect was off the charts? Momma was contacted by the school and was asked if I could attend Hunter Model School, which was especially for gifted children.

"*Ahv cuz not*" (of course not), said Momma. She would have had to take me there every day on the subway. So there goes the myth of how Jewish parents wanted the "best" for their children.

My whole life was spent reading, and the highlight of my young life was when I was given a card to the adult section of the library. I would take out the maximum number of books and hide additional ones behind other books.

I lived at home until I got my working papers at the age of sixteen and then started to look for jobs. My skills were negligible and I was a runt, so I took whatever I could get. Believe me, I was on the bottom of the food chain.

Pin curls were my specialty, and my friends would count on my expertise. I would get invited to many sleepovers just so I was present to do their hair. Therefore, I decided to go to the local beauty shops and tell them of my particular skills. The owners laughed uproariously and asked me when was the last time I looked in a mirror.

I took the hint and devoted more time looking in the classi-fieds. Finally, I took a very low-paying job working for a large book publisher. It was totally boring so I started shooting rubber bands across the office. Then I went to work for Fruit of the Loom in the men's underwear department. Sometimes I would stuff leftover lunch into the jockey shorts. I was not appreciated there either.

THE WAR
by Lou Polley

When my father came home at midday on Sunday, December 7, 1941, with a grave expression on his face, he turned on the radio, and I knew that something serious was about to happen.

Then we heard President Roosevelt's voice. "My friends, the Japanese have bombed Pearl Harbor this morning. Our country is at war." Our usually stoic parents began to cry. They had three sons, ages twenty-two, nineteen, and fifteen. The oldest brother left his pre-med studies and enlisted in the U.S. Army Air Corps. He became first pilot on the Air Force's B-17 and B-24. My parents, my fifteen-year-old brother, and I drove from Illinois to San Antonio, Texas, for his graduation ceremony. We were so proud of our handsome pilot in his blue uniform with the silver wings pinned on it. A year later his plane went down on a mission from South America to North Africa. We would never see our handsome pilot again.

Meanwhile, the nineteen-year-old joined the Sea Bees and was sent to the South Pacific. The fifteen-year-old joined an ROTC program. When his reserve group was deployed to participate in the Battle of the Bulge, he was barely seventeen. He survived, though most of his company did not.

Patriotism ran high! We, at home, supported our troops with letters written on airmail paper, which was very thin so as not to take up room or add weight to the planes delivering them. Often the replies were censored with heavy black marks through them so that the enemy could not gain any information about the movement of the troops

We had ration books for gasoline, rubber tires, shoes, sugar, and butter. The auto industry did not produce new cars. They made planes instead. Nylon stockings were not available. Nylon was being used for parachutes. Everyone who had a backyard planted a victory garden. Canned and processed food was saved for the troops. Jobs were plentiful. "Rosie the Riveter" became the theme song for many women who went to work in the munitions factories.

Silk banners with a gold star in the center hung in windows, including ours, signifying that a husband or brother had been lost in the war. "I'll Be Home for Christmas If Only In My Dreams" described the holiday mood during the war years. One popular war song that always brought tears to my eyes was "Off We Go Into the Wild Blue Yonder," the U.S. Army Air Force song.

LEAVING CHINA
by Stella Mah

Part I

When we started school in the fall of 1949, the Kuomintang was in power. Everything changed in a couple of months when the Communists came into Shanghai one night. We lived in the suburbs and neither saw nor heard any fighting. The next morning, Mom went out as usual to shop but turned right around and came home. She told us not to go to school that morning as the whole business district was closed, and people were dressed in very somber clothing.

We stayed home for a few days to wait and see. When we did return to school we were told that we would have most classes as before, but we needed to wait for new text books for reading and history. Those new texts contained Communist political history, and the stories were about farmers' struggles under oppressive landowners. We had to change our currency before we could buy anything. It was as if a new country had been dropped on us.

In the final years of the Kuomintang, inflation was so rampant that people went back to silver coins of an earlier period. They were called "big heads" and "small heads." The difference was the silver content. Mom would take a few big heads and change them to small heads and also use inflated paper money to do her shopping. The exchange rate varied from day to day so one only changed enough cash to cover that day's shopping. Mom carried the stacks of cash in a cloth shopping bag. When the Communists no longer permitted the use of the big and small heads, we had to adjust quickly to the new currency, the *renminbe*, which means "people's money."

Dad's health was improving, but he was still lethargic and living day by day. Mom, however, saw the handwriting on the wall and persuaded him to leave China before the government closed the country. They devised a way to smuggle our British passports to a cousin in Hong Kong. Then Dad and Brother took the train to Canton, our hometown.

Among the Chinese at that time, your hometown was the home of your ancestors. It had nothing to do with where you were born. For example, my family is Cantonese even though Mom, Brother, and I were born in Shanghai and Dad was born in Hong Kong.

If Dad were asked why he was leaving Shanghai, he would say that he was going home, a very understandable sentiment to another Chinese. From Canton it was only a quick train ride to the border of Hong Kong, which at that time was open to Cantonese. Once in Hong Kong, Dad would retrieve their British passports and could travel to wherever he could find a job. But the money he was hoping to receive from his best friend, Pan, did not arrive, and Pan ignored Dad's telegrams and registered letters. Dad had to scramble to borrow money to live.

Dad and Brother left in the spring, probably April or May 1950. The plan was for Mom and me to follow. Well, all the best-laid plans were for naught when the Korean War broke out in June 1950. All radio news and newspapers were censored, so we had no idea of what was happening. Dad had asked a very good friend and colleague, an Englishman, and his Russian wife, to look out for us as long as they remained in Shanghai. But they were being evicted from China by the Communist government so they told us that we should leave too.

Again, we packed a few necessities in two suitcases and traveled by train to Canton as Dad had done a few months earlier. Mom took what cash we had. One did not go to the bank to withdraw money. It would attract too much attention.

The train journey took three full days. We arrived at the border, now the booming city of Shenzen. Back in those days, it was just a tiny village where the train tracks from the north ended. We had brought some hand luggage for our three-day journey. Mom found a coolie to take the hand luggage to the border, which was over rough unpaved hilly land and took about thirty minutes to cross. The coolie and I had to straddle rusty train tracks and climb up and down slopes while Mom went to retrieve our luggage from the storage train. I was given the job of following the coolie because I could keep up with him as he jogged with our hand luggage on the two ends of a pole.

I waited with the coolie for Mom at the customs shed, but she did not come. The coolie wanted to be paid, but I had no money. Other passengers came and went. Some said they saw Mom with our suitcases looking for a coolie. Some of the customs officials began to tease me, a child of eleven. They told me that Mom had abandoned me because I was a girl and not worth the bother. They said the coolie must be paid, and if Mom did not pay him, he would sell me. Fortunately, I knew I was loved, and Mom would never abandon me. I was trying to keep up a calm front, but internally I was racked with fear. I had no money and no documentation. How was I going to get to Hong Kong?

No passengers appeared for a long stretch. The customs officers started their haranguing again. I decided I must search for Mom and persuaded the coolie to come along, promising him that she would pay him three times what he was initially promised to make up for his loss in time. There must have been conviction in my voice, because he did what I asked. We went back and forth between the customs shed and the train several times, but we could not find Mom. The last time a porter told me that everybody had left, I was very close to tears, but did not let any flow. I told the coolie that I could call my relatives in Hong Kong to bring money for him. This was a lie, as I did not know the phone numbers. He was very impatient with me as he had lost half a day of wages and was stuck with this pesky child who would not let him out of her sight.

At last, three hours had gone by since our train arrived. When we walked back to the customs shed, I heard Mom's voice calling for me. I couldn't see her as we were on different sides of a hill, but I could hear her, and scrambled up the hill. She looked so small in that setting, all alone at the bottom of the sandy rocky hill. I did not cry but just ran into her arms and hugged her hard. She told me that she had been shouting my pet name for the last couple of hours, going back and forth over that rugged no-man's land.

I gathered my wits and returned to the business at hand. I told Mom that I had promised the coolie three times the money she had negotiated with him initially. She paid him, plus a tip, and he took off quite happily. The customs officer, a young woman, told Mom that I had been poised and never showed any fear of having been abandoned. She asked Mom how I could be so sure and confessed that, if she had been in my shoes, she would have been very frightened. If only she knew.

Part II

We left China just in time. The Communists had been in Shanghai about half a year when Dad and Brother left. The Communists had been taking over the interior of China ever since the end of WWII. Before WWII, the two opposing parties, the Kuomintang and the Communists, had decided to put aside their differences to combat their common enemy, the Japanese. As soon as the war was over, the civil war reignited.

In the countryside, where most of the poor—the farmers and laborers—were, the Communists were enthusiastically welcomed and they had a relatively easy time taking over. Once they had caught the landlords, business owners, and village leaders, the Communists officials took control. Their progress was slowed, however, by their lack of money for arms, food, clothing, transportation, and other necessities. And, of course, they lacked military training. But they made up for their deficiencies by their determination, dedication, and willingness to sacrifice themselves for their cause.

In the meantime, the Kuomintang, under the corrupt leadership of Chiang Kai-Shek, was desperate for help. The United States supported his government because it feared Communism. Unfortunately, Chiang, a military man, was a weak political leader and had corrupt people around him. His government, like a big sluggish lava flow, just slid into chaos. All the powerful leaders found ways to move their assets and families out the country and allowed the country to be taken by the Communists.

When the Communists entered Shanghai, the most sophisticated and largest city at that time, there was very little fighting. They took over the whole city in one night, finding no resistance from the nationalists. After a short period of adjustment, the local city slickers found out that many of the officials were really country-folk who were not very well educated. They were overwhelmed by the size and the complexity of the city. These city slickers ran circles around the mid-level officials who, besides a lack of sophistication to handle the locals, also feared to make decisions on their own. For a while, about twelve to eighteen months, government continued as before. The Communists were putting their political philosophy before all else, slogans appeared on walls, schoolbooks were changed, currency was changed. To involve the populace, petition booths appeared all over the place. Each booth tried to get as many signatures as possible for whatever its cause. On my daily walk to and from school, I would encounter at least two to three booths, all trying to get signatures from passersby. I would sign all of them, using the opportunity to practice different signatures until I settled on one I liked!

Travel restrictions were not yet put in place. That was why we got away. Many of my parents' friends were a little slow to move. They were trapped in the country for the next twenty-five years. Among those trapped were my in-laws. My father-in-law had a thriving business with his brother in imports and exports. They had several offices around the country, including an office in Hong Kong. They had agents around the world. My father-in-law was a very astute man. He sent his only son, my husband, aged fifteen, to Hong Kong to a boarding school. He and his wife planned to leave China as soon as he had sorted out the loose ends of their business. Unfortunately for him and his brother, they took a little too long. The gates of the Chinese Dragon were slammed shut. As successful entrepreneurs, they were the most despised by the Communists. He and his brother were put under house arrest to write their confessions. They had separate Spartan rooms so they could not collude. Every day, an official would check on their writings. They were encouraged to confess their own "sins" but also to implicate anybody else who might be flying below the Communist radar.

The pressure on them was horrendous. They had to be very careful before committing pen to paper. They could not scratch out anything. Every scrap of paper had to be turned in for examination. Then, every week, they were subjected to two to three hours of interrogation in which they might be questioned about something they wrote a month or more ago. My father-in-law was under house arrest for several months. He and his brother were found guilty of treating their employees badly and they were imprisoned for several months. Theirs was relatively light punishment.

Every employer had disgruntled employees, and these people had a field day denouncing their bosses. Any slight or reprimand was deemed an offense. Before long, there were too many guilty people to put in jail. They devised a new form of punishment. The "guilty" were taken out to public places where they knelt before their accusers to confess their sins. The men had their guilt tied on their foreheads with headbands. The crowd would jeer, shout obscenities, or throw stones or feces at the prisoners. Sometimes the attacks escalated to riots before the soldiers regained control. After such treatment, many men were completely broken. Some committed suicide; others became catatonic and mere shadows of themselves. A man who worked under my dad was questioned so intensively that he jumped from a fourth-floor window. He lived some years after the attempted suicide and was crippled for life.

It is hard for me to think of how many people suffered in similar ways. These incidents I mention here are related to people my family actually knew. The majority of those who were really deserving of such treatment found their way out of the country, and most of those remaining were the mid-level bosses, who did not deserve their punishment. Those who survived and had lived under the Communist regime for a quarter century never mention today the atrocities they suffered.

THE BOX
by Nancy Braund-Boruch

I did something this past week that I have not done for years. I opened the box. And IT began again. And I can't shove IT back.

Let me back up a bit. My great-nephew, Matt Braund, turned sixteen last week. For his birthday present, I drove him from Louisville to Chicago so we could have several days just by ourselves without his parents or siblings—a bonding time, as he called it. I had done this for his brother, Nick, a few years before. We "did" the lakefront, Michigan Avenue, my gym, NikeTown, and more. We also went on a tour of the Great Lakes Naval Station and what is left of Fort Sheridan. Matt says he might go into the service after high school. The U.S. Marine Corps is his first choice, the U.S. Army, his second. In Matt's case, both his mom and I think the service might be a good idea, despite his father's, and all of our, understandable fears.

Touring the naval base brought back memories for me, and many questions for Matt. When we saw models of the WWII aircraft carriers, Matt asked about his great-granddad, my father, who had been a Navy chaplain on the USS Bon Homme Richard in the Pacific. Later, at another exhibit, he asked if I had known any Marines. I turned away and paused before saying, "Yes. Many." Then I turned back and told him that, after the war, his great-granddad went into the Navy Reserves and that his assignment had been as chaplain to the Marines at 8th and I Streets, the Marine Corps headquarters in DC. I left it at that.

Saturday, the night before we had to drive back to Louisville, Matt again asked if I knew any Marines. Again I hesitated and turned away. About an hour later, I went into the crawl space and came out with an old plastic box—the pre-Rubbermaid kind. It was filled with papers. We sat on the bed and I pulled out a large black-and-white photo of a good-looking man in a uniform.

"Who is that?" Matt asked.

"Major Walter Michael Murphy, USMC, 1st Battalion, 1st Marines, 1st Marine Division. He was my boyfriend. I met him when he was a captain at The Basic School in Quantico. I was a graduate student at Georgetown."

"Where is he now?"

"He was killed January 31, 1968, in Viet Nam—in Hue during the Tet Offensive. Killed the day before your great-granddad died of a heart attack. Here are some of Walt's letters to me; these are four I wrote to him before I got notification of his death. As you see, they came back stamped Return to Sender. Here are other photos and newspaper clippings, and letters to me from his buddies and from the top brass. These are from his brother and mother."

"How old was he?" Matt asked.

"Thirty-two. I was twenty-five. He'd be seventy-five this coming September. War is not pretty, Matt. Being a service man or woman is not easy. With the good comes the sad." I closed the box.

"Were you proud of him?" Matt asked.

"Yes. I was proud that he did what he chose to do. I loved him. And I will be proud of you, and I will always love you whatever you decide to do in life."

The papers and photos were put away, but now all of IT is loose again—Viet Nam, the protests, Nixon, Watergate, student riots—the body bags, the lost innocence, the lost youth, the lost generation. I am now forced to re-examine them. IT cannot be put back into the box so easily.

CHICAGO PARK CITY
by Deanne Thompson

Listening to the news about all the tragic shootings and disasters going on this year in and around Chicago reminded me of something that happened to me as a teenager. Life as I knew it wasn't dangerous back then, and my friends and I were allowed to get on the "L" and ride to the south side of Chicago to Park City. I loved skating to the organ music and skating with the boys. Afterward we would go down the street, get White Castle hamburgers, and eat them on the L ride home.

One evening a neighbor of mine wanted to go skating and, as always, I was anxious to skate. When we got to the skating rink, I didn't see any of my old friends, but my neighbor saw her boyfriend and wanted to talk to him. I had my doubts about him. He seemed a little on the rough side. She wanted to leave and begged me to go with her to his house. I didn't want to go but I didn't want to ride the L home alone. I agreed, and around the corner to his place we went. When we got there, he introduced one of his friends to me. Talk about sleazy. I was ready to leave. I was almost to the station when I heard her call me to wait up for her. She was really "salty" that I left and wasn't ready to go home yet. I told her, "Too bad," and if she wanted to stay, not to let me stop her. She begged me to go back with her, but I stuck to my decision and continued to the L and we rode home in silence.

The next day, the most chilling thing happened. I'll never forget this as long as I live. I was thumbing through the newspaper the next day and an article caught my eye—"Police Found Girl Murdered." They had apprehended the suspects. Right there in black-and-white print were my neighbor's boyfriend's and his friend's names. We never found out what happened after that. I don't know if they were guilty, convicted, or what happened to them, but I did believe they were capable of doing such a thing, especially if they were drinking. My neighbor was so shaken, I don't think she went skating after that.

ONE SUMMER DAY
by Pat Lee

It was 1954, a warm Friday afternoon. We were heading home to Grand Rapids for the weekend in Keith's new Studebaker. My roommate Carol was in the back seat. She and I were both attending an eight-week summer school session at Western Michigan University. My two courses would give me the six hours credit I needed for a temporary teaching certificate. That May, I had been hired by the school board—two farmers and a general store owner—to teach for a year in the one-room school house on Four Mile Road. Working that year would earn the money I needed to finish my last two years of college at the University of Michigan in Ann Arbor, a dream come true. Keith had a dream, too. He wanted to be a doctor, though he had never even been to college. At the time, he was working as a paint sprayer at the Steelcase Corporation, a job he hated.

On the Beltway, skirting my hometown, we came to a four-way stop. I looked across the intersection and saw the lights change. As we moved forward, a car turned left into our path. Keith wasn't driving fast, but he couldn't stop in time. For me it was all in slow motion. Keith pushed me to the floor. We crashed. I heard the windshield shatter. My roommate had been launched into it, and when I looked up I saw her bloody face and its imprint on the shattered windshield. There were no seat belts then.

I was untouched except for a cut on my finger. It would take three days for the shock to kick in. Keith wasn't hurt physically, but his face told another story. He got to the hospital emergency room before I did, and when I got there I saw him standing against a white wall staring at Carol on a table. She wasn't moving. He was quiet, helpless. I stood next to him watching his face.

I don't remember whether Carol's parents appeared then. I don't think so. The emergency room staff told Keith and I that the best plastic surgeon they had was on his way. He could repair Carol's face so the scarring would be minimal. Some days later in their home, Carol's parents told us in detail about their daughter's earlier surgeries to correct various vision problems. They told us they might sue Keith. When we left their house, I was scared, but I told him not to worry. We would get a lawyer. I remember becoming fierce and focused. I knew Keith's background. I knew his struggle. I knew he was undeserving of more pain and sorrow. And I knew how he was suffering over Carol's injury. We didn't know any lawyers, but I found one fast, perhaps in the yellow pages. His office was downtown. He saw us. We told our story. He took the case and contacted Carol's parents. They did not sue.

Carol began to heal. Seeing me was painful for her. Maybe she returned to school, but I'm not sure. I did return and got those six credits. Keith and I saw each other for another five years. My mother said, only once, "This is the man you should marry, Pat." I would regret that I didn't. I got my degree, and Keith, after many years, became a doctor. I never saw Carol again.

HANS FELL
by Ruth Granick

Hans had grown up in Vienna, and part of his school work was rappelling. He climbed mountains, he skied, he ice skated. When we visited Vienna, he showed me where he had ice skated and pointed out the spot where Sonja Henie had practiced.

Some years later we were visiting Hans's younger daughter, Candida, in Washington State. She, her husband, and two sons walked out with us. It was a beautiful spot. We were walking up a slight incline when Hans fell. Suddenly, no outcry. He got up as gracefully and quickly as possible, and we continued our walk.

Back home in the Midwest we had arrived early for a gig at Selfhelp, a retirement home. When we walked over to a nearby park, Hans fell. I was alone with him, had very little strength in my arms, didn't know what to do, so I said, "Oh," in a woeful voice. He let me know, very gently, that I was "not to worry about him," that he would indeed rise. This time he was very slow at getting himself up. We went to the gig and did well, as always.

One day he phoned me from a hospital. He'd awakened, unable to move most of his body. Fortunately his phone was within reach and he dialed 911 for an ambulance. When he returned home he researched retirement homes. He wanted to live in my area and chose the King Home because the medical director there promised to treat Hans's essential tremor.

Then came the move. Four Wur kids, Hans's adult children, came to his apartment where they went over his music and books, each choosing what he or she could use. When they'd chosen the music they wanted, they turned to me, suggesting that I select some scores, which I did.

Hans moved into the King Home and became seriously depressed. We did a program in their auditorium and were very well received. But Hans's depression progressed. The medical director denied he'd promised to treat the essential tremor, which grew worse. When he could no longer play the piano to his satisfaction, Hans refused to do any more of our programs.

Hans, my wonderful, cultured lover, was getting lost. Little by little, all that meant something to him, that gave his life meaning, became more and more difficult, and he gave up.

The physical therapy room at the King Home was well equipped, but Hans refused to use it. When I suggested that they try to seduce him into exercising, I was told very brusquely that they did not force their clients to do anything. Hans no longer fell. He ate in his room, slept most of the time. He got a little bit better when I took him to a good doctor who discovered a serious thyroid problem and medicated it. When I asked the King Home nurse whether he was getting his Synthroid, the nurse yelled at me, "You don't trust us." "No, I don't," I replied. "He's had serious thyroid deficiency since he entered the King Home, and none of you even noticed it."

Hans was later moved to a very well-run physical therapy center at the Presbyterian Home but, by that time, he had given up. He lay in bed waiting to die. The King Home appointed a psychiatrist who saw him once a week or so. After half a year, the man told me he had not been able to establish any contact with Hans.

Hans had been the joy of my life, my lover, my companion, my accompanist, my everything. Slowly I was losing him, and I mourned him long before he died. Felix, Hans's older son, took him to his home in Albuquerque. There was no radio, CD player, or TV in his room. When I visited, the young woman sitting with him brought him an omelet, and walked away. The omelet was all in one piece. His tremor made it impossible for him to cut it, so he said he wasn't hungry. I cut it up for him and he finished it.

Alex, Hans's younger son, phoned me one day and told me that Hans had died. He said Hans would be cremated and his ashes scattered on a mountain. Hans loved mountains.

Hans no longer falls.

AN INCREDIBLE JOURNEY
by Lou Polley

Autumn of 2007 was a season of travel for me, flying to Santa Barbara in October, to Michigan for Thanksgiving, then to Vancouver for Christmas and finally to Whistler Mountain for New Years. When my son dropped me off at my apartment in Evanston on January 4, 2008, I was pretty exhausted and wasted no time getting ready for bed, which felt wonderfully warm and cozy after being away for so many weeks. Suddenly I found that nature was calling. My legs were numb and wouldn't support me. Before I realized what was happening, I found myself on the floor and the bathroom seemed miles away.

"Ring, ring." I heard my phone ringing and, though I knew where it was, I couldn't reach it. "Ring, ring." There it was again. "I must answer it and let someone know that I am having trouble," I thought, but again, my legs wouldn't move. Panic began to overtake me. "I'm going to die right here on the floor, and when someone finds me it will be too late."

Suddenly I wasn't on the floor any more. Instead I was in a beautiful snow-covered mountainous landscape. "Must be the Italian Alps," I thought. A wedding was in progress, and I was one of the guests. The bride's family was carrying silk banners, as was the groom's. A funny little man, whose name was George, was driving a cart that had skis instead of wheels. He delivered the groom's family to the ceremony and then went back for the bride's.

It was very cold. My hands were freezing. The father of the groom gave me a pair of fur-lined Italian leather gloves. I gave them back when the groom's mother said they were family heirlooms. I kept asking where the bathroom was, but no one would tell me. A brides-maid, Diana, was assigned to help me find a bathroom, but Diana was chasing after the groom and had no time for me. I was beginning to feel self-conscious about my green cloth coat, for the other guests wore long fur coats and fur-lined boots. George kept driving around in his ski cart, which was decorated with twinkling lights, delivering guests and presents.

Finally, after much pomp and waving of the colorful banners, the ceremony concluded, followed by a huge banquet set out in the best Italian style. The father of the groom invited me back to the groom's house to wait until George had time to take me to the airport for the trip home. I was amazed to find that my son and daughter-in-law were there, stretched out on white Italian leather couches and asleep. It seems they had come to accompany me home, though I had no idea how they had found out where I was.

I asked if I could use the laundry room to freshen up clothes before starting home. While I was doing my laundry, a door opened and someone began shouting, "Mom! Mom!"

"Must be the Italian children coming home from school," I thought.

But then I heard it again, louder and more familiar. It was my daughter. Next I heard my son-in-law's voice saying, "Don't worry, Mom. Help is on the way."

I was traveling again, this time in an ambulance to a hospital. While in Italy, three days had gone by.

MARY
by Barbara Gazzolo

Occasionally I wonder about Mary, where she is now, whether her young mother is still living. It is six years now since I last saw Mary. She was only one year old and hugging a stuffed toy dog.

Mary and her mother had been given shelter at the church center in Soweto, South Africa. They took their meals with us in the dining room. In fact, it was in that dining room one day that we saw this little brown girl pull herself up on a chair and launch herself on her first steps. It may have frightened her, certainly startled her, as we all broke out in cheers and applause.

There were over twenty of us from the Chicago area. We had volunteered to build an AIDS clinic in Soweto. We lived and worked behind high metal fences, watching the clinic rise one cement block at a time. We were housed in a hostel once built to shelter runaway anti-apartheid activists. Now it housed out-of-towners in Soweto on church business. It was not the Ramada Inn, but the single beds were good enough for tired builders, and the chef prepared really good meals. He worked hard in that kitchen but kept his spirits up by disappearing some weekends to visit his wives and children in Kwa Zulu.

We were too busy unloading and hauling cement blocks, making cement, and raising clinic walls to see much of Mary or her mother except at meals. It seems that during the day, Rose, Mary's mother, made bead pins of black, green, and yellow to sell in the market to tourists. Now that Mary was walking, she needed shoes, and I gave Rose money to buy them. That evening she shyly approached me and returned the money. She hadn't been able to find shoes for Mary.

The clinic buildings were assuming shape as piles of earth and stones grew around their bases. In the evening after dinner, there were always builders gathered to drink and gossip together under the moon. They piled several cement blocks as chairs and leaned against the hostel wall. Some had been working since dawn; it was cooler to work early because by noon the sun was scorching.

One evening I joined the friends for some wine and talk and noticed that Mary's mother was standing several feet away from us, attending but not wanting to intrude. She motioned me over and I joined her in the shadows of the night. Mary's mother, Rose, was a pretty woman about eighteen years old. Like many women, she had no husband to help care for her and her little daughter. For a while now she had found refuge at the church headquarters. It could only be temporary.

For some reason she needed to share something that night. "My mother and father died when I was twelve," she told me. "1 had no way to live and had to go out on the streets," she almost whispered. "That's how I got HIV."

And that's how you got Mary, I thought to myself. Eighteen, alone, with HIV and a little girl to rear. She looked up at me. I don't know what she hoped I would do or say, but without any reflection I asked, "Has Mary been checked? Does she have HIV?" Her mother shook her head. She had asked someone about it and had been dismissed. They told her to come back when Mary was older. Older, I thought. I'm no medic, but it seemed to me that the sooner Mary could be diagnosed the better. Didn't they care?

"We're taking you both to the hospital tomorrow," I said, sure someone could drive us to Jo'burg's hospital the next day after breakfast. And so we went. Dewey and I borrowed a van and made our way into Johannesburg with Mary and her mother. We didn't say a lot on the way. The hospital was modern and open to all, no color lines. Up the elevator we went, Rose mute with anxiety, cuddling Mary in her arms,

As Dewey and I waited, a social worker interviewed Rose and a nurse took some of Mary's blood. There were no answers when they returned to us. "The tests will be back tomorrow," we were told, and there was no choice but to leave and await the outcome. We drove home to Soweto. At least the little girl had been tested.

First thing the next day, we left in the morning for the hospital and some answers, all of us anxious. But when we returned to the second floor clinic we were bluntly denied. "It's Saturday and only the social worker who did yesterday's interview can give you the test results," the nurse told us.

Dewey exploded. "Give me the phone," he roared. "I want to talk to the hospital administrator." Dialing the administrator, he handed me the phone. "I'm too angry to be rational. You do the talking." He left the room to walk fast anywhere. So I found myself talking to the hospital administrator, who carefully explained hospital policy and the need for it. Why did they promise answers "tomorrow" and not give them?

The three of us, Rose holding Mary, and I, walked numbly to the elevator. Someone knew Mary's fate and it wasn't us. Dewey greeted us downstairs. He had assuaged his frustration and rage by buying Mary an enormous stuffed toy dog and a bottle of juice at the gift shop. We drove back in silence.

It made it harder for us knowing that on Sunday, the next day, we would be flying out. We couldn't take them back to the hospital on Monday. Fortunately, we were able to persuade Tim, the Habitat for Humanity man, to make the run on Monday.

A week or so later an e-mail from Africa brought the news. Mary is clear. What a relief, but occasionally I can't help but wonder about Mary—where she is now, how she is doing, and whether her young mother is still living.

PELICANS
by Penelope Whiteside

Some lay like sculptures in the mud. Some were hunkered down, eyes dulled by the dark ooze that coated them. I saw those pelicans on the evening news. They were drenched in oil, innocent victims of an ecological disaster, the BP oil spill in the Gulf of Mexico. How could they possibly understand it? How pitiable their attempts to clean themselves off, to raise their hopeless wings in flight.

Normally, I think of pelicans as somewhat comical-looking birds. If winged creatures held beauty contests, they would get the booby prize. Perhaps their lack of beauty and utter originality of design are what make them endearing. I have treasured a pelican ornament, which I bought seventeen years ago in New Orleans. It was the last time my widowed father, my brothers and sister-in-law, my boys, and Bob and I had Christmas together. That ornament represents the brown pelican of the Gulf Coast; it is sculpted in papier-mâché and painted. Like the bird itself, it is a little too heavy. It has weighed down the branch of every Christmas tree since. Every year, it lays somewhere in the middle branches where the tree can best support it.

This last winter, the pelican stayed in a box with the other ornaments, unused. I did not purchase a tree because I spent Christmas in Florida. From the beach in front of my north Naples rental right on the Gulf, I could watch actual pelicans flying in groups low along the shore. Hordes of them would appear all at once, resting on the sand. On another day, they might be gone entirely. One or two would flap their heavy wings and then suddenly dive straight downward, emerging with a fish. Then they would flip their catch out of their enormous craws through the air into their throats. Other seabirds buzzed around in case they missed.

Long before I ever saw a live pelican I imagined one, having read a poem by Lamartine. That French poet immortalized a mother pelican who gave her hungry babies her own flesh to eat. For Christians receiving the sanctified bread at the Eucharistic table, Jesus says, "This is my body." In medieval times, the pelican image was an allegory for Christ.

Pelican as mother, pelican as God, pelican as the ugly one in the bird kingdom.

I cannot grasp the scope of the environmental disaster. There are many human beings and other forms of life vastly affected by it, of course. Yet, what makes me weep is the sight of those oil-drenched pelicans.

MAPPING THE
WORLD

A WHOLE NEW WORLD
by Stella Mah

England in 1946 was very short of food. Staying in the Strand Palace provided little nourishment, especially as we did not care for English cuisine. Before long we went to Zurich, which was Dad's real destination.

We had an English governess who tutored us in English and took care of us while Dad and Mom dealt with social and business activities. Miss Frost was a big woman, about thirty years old. She had a beautiful face and lovely complexion, the well-known English peaches-and-cream complexion. Her body was huge. When we sent out our laundry at the hotel one day, Miss Frost's panties ended up with our things. I remember holding up this huge pair of knickers and wondering whose they were. Suddenly I heard my brother shout with glee. He snatched the underwear from me and waved it in the air. It ballooned out like a parachute. You can be sure Miss Frost was not pleased.

We soon moved to a pension, a residential inn. This was a more suitable accommodation than the Strand Palace, and the food in Switzerland was much better. We had lessons, all in English, five mornings a week. We went out for walks after lunch every day and then did homework until tea time, which was our dinner. Even though we were Chinese and were in Switzerland, we followed the English custom because, after all, Miss Frost was English.

Our parents probably liked having us tucked away early in the evenings while they had an opportunity to do adult things. Dad had to travel around continental Europe, and Mom stayed with us until my brother recovered from surgery. I think Miss Frost was with us for about three months, roughly one term of school or a trimester. She despaired of my spelling, comparing me with my brother, who took great pleasure in learning to spell long difficult words. I think he learned to spell Czechoslovakia, the longest word in the atlas of

Europe, just to show off. We could understand simple English by the time she returned to England. Today I am so grateful for spell-check.

Dad and Mom decided we really needed to be with other children, and as they had to do some traveling, they sent us to a boarding school for children of diplomats or other non-Swiss nationals. They were told that the school had about thirty to forty students and, when they visited the school during summer vacation, there was indeed a large group of children. But during regular term, there were only three of us. After a couple of weeks my parents returned to take us out for lunch. We ate like refugees. They asked us probing questions and found out that we had had no lessons and that there was only one other child, Margaret, and a mademoiselle who took us out for walks.

As soon as possible, we were moved to a different boarding school up in the Alps. The place was run by an English couple, Mr. and Mrs. Gissing, who had three children of their own. The excellent air was very good for my brother, who had a lung infection following measles. Our lessons were scheduled; we were served plain but nutritious food and enjoyed plenty of fresh air. A goat herder came down from the high grazing field to see us because he had never seen a Chinese person before. We could not converse as he spoke a Swiss dialect, but he and my brother became friends.

One day Mr. Gissing asked my brother and me if our father smoked opium. My imperfect understanding of English led me to reply, "Mom smokes but not Dad." I got a most peculiar look from Mr. Gissing. My brother, who understood English better and knew what opium was, quickly said, "Mom smoked cigarettes, and neither of our parents smoked opium."

Dad and Mom came periodically to visit us and brought us goodies. While they were away, they made sure that we received a parcel of Swiss chocolates every week.

We were in Switzerland for about a year and then we returned to England. This time we rented a house, 11 Durham Road, Raynes Park, just outside of London in the county of Surrey. We went to Ridgeway School, a co-ed school, which was unusual in England. We walked to the bus stop by ourselves to take the bus back and forth. We were almost eight and ten years old.

My brother and I were introduced to the school population after their morning assembly. The headmaster said our names, our ages, and which classes we would be going to. Finally, he said we came from China. The pupils' assignment that day would be to look in an atlas for the country of China. The girls in my class were very friendly to me, and I did not feel any discrimination. There was a boy, however, who, for some reason, did not like me and got me kicked off the Christmas Sing at the dress rehearsal. As you can imagine, I was very upset, especially as my parents were coming to the show. Anyway, I took matters into my own hands. At the performance, I went up on stage with everyone and sang three hymns. Thinking back, I am surprised by own chutzpah. Also, I can't imagine a teacher kicking a seven-year-old out of a Christmas Sing because she did not know all the words to one of the hymns. Was this subtle discrimination?

The house we rented was very different from anything we had known. It had three floors and five bedrooms. There was a dining room, which we only used once, when we had guests for Christmas. There was a larder way in the back of the kitchen. It remained dark and cool all year. We used it as cool storage, as very few families had refrigerators or iceboxes. Mom learned to make pies and other desserts, which were foreign to us, so she made them only occasionally. She cooked Chinese-style food, which we ate with potatoes or bread since rice was not available and pasta was unheard of. Everything was rationed. We received little coupon books, one per person, which allowed us to buy limited quantities of meat, sugar, and eggs—one per person per week. My brother received an extra egg because of his poor health.

Mom, ever ingenious, saw that the butcher left a lot of meat on the bones because bones were not rationed. She cooked stews and soups from those meaty bones, which were delicious. Chickens were expensive in terms of coupons, but once Mom noticed that the butcher cut off the wingtips and feet of chickens and tossed the organs. Mom asked him for them and cooked up wonderful dishes for us. Finally the butcher asked Mom what she did with the scraps he tossed. Did she have a dog? She decided to take him a bowl of her stew, and he could not believe how good it was. In those days, the technique of stir-fry cooking was not known in England, and Mom gave him some stir-fried chicken liver and several recipes. He was astounded that chicken liver could be so delicious. From then on, he saved her very meaty bones.

I recall that we could buy ice cream only once a week, and a limited quantity of candy. Because we did not crave candy like the English, we were able to trade coupons with neighbors. Clothing, shoes, blankets, sheets, and other items were all rationed. Those years after the war were very lean times.

COLLEGE AND WAY BEYOND
by Beata Hayton

I started at the University of Chicago during World War II. I was
assigned to Kelly Hall, a dormitory where they served meals. My
roommate's father was a professor in Israel, and her parents ran a
summer camp in Maine. Since I was at least a nominal Catholic, I put
a crucifix on one side of the door and she put a mezuzah on the other.
By 1941, the Army took the dorm over, and four of us moved over
to Gates where you had to cook your own food. Because we often
made meals from the Russian war relief cookbook, some of the other
students thought we were very odd.

Then the Army took over Gates, and I moved to International
House. I met African-Americans for the first time, middle-class as
I was, but graduate students and a lot smarter than I. And I hung
out with some guys who liked to try out different neighborhood restaurants for dinner. Then the Army took over I-House too, and my
friends and I rented an apartment in a two-flat on Ingleside Avenue.
Some of the army guys on campus came by because it was so home-
like. One boy, Philip, left his violin there so he could practice once
in a while.

One of my pleasures in college was writing a gossip column for
the college newspaper, the *Maroon*. After college, I went to work
for the City News Bureau. Because I'd always been nosey, it was a
great place for me to work. We covered police news—mostly rob-
beries, burglaries, accidents, court hearings (mainly divorces), and
the county building. It was a wonderful way to learn how the city
worked. One night at home, I got a call from the night-desk man
asking me to go to one of the north side police stations to cover a crucifixion. The cops had answered a call and found this man, his hands
neatly nailed to a cross and a crown of thorns on his head. At the top
of the cross was a note saying, "Follow this good man, the brother of
Jesus Christ." They took him down, took him to the hospital, figured

he was promoting some Nazi-type movement, and charged him with disorderly conduct. He was fined in court the next day.

I was too timid to apply to any of the newspapers for work and, when the war ended and the men came back, I was out of a job. I ended up in New York, living with my sister's friend, Margaret Harrison, and working at the same hospital fund-raising firm that she did. I called Hall Overton, the guy I'd been dating in Chicago, and he came to New York. He was a composer, a jazz musician, and great on the piano.

That ended me on a six-month tour of Africa with my sister, promoted and paid for by my mother. She had grown up in an era before the Musicians' Union, and I think she was afraid that she and my father would end up supporting Hall and me. *Es gibt Leuten und Musikanten* was the old German expression she used. Translation: There are people and there are musicians.

Anyways, Wilhelmina and I took off for Africa with my mother's missionary cousin, Myrtle Zaffke, who was going back to her mission station after a year of postwar leave. We flew to Leopoldville, now Kinshasa, then travelled up the Congo River on an old sidewheeler to Stanleyville, now Kisangani. Then we travelled by car to cousin Myrtle's mission station in Usumbura, Ruanda-Urundi. Wilhelmina and I stayed with her at first, but we both smoked and the other missionaries didn't approve, so we moved into a hotel in town.

We moved on, I think by train, to Nairobi, which was a pretty big modern town in comparison with Usumbura. Then we went to Zanzibar, a wonderful little island off the coast where the air was always fragrant with the cinnamon and cloves that grew there. The town was wonderful. Streets were lined with old stone buildings with great, carved wooden doors. We stayed in a bed-and-breakfast a family friend had recommended. The owners were very nice and tried to be sure we got food we liked. Basically, they made a living from their bar. Muslims aren't supposed to drink but some did, and they could get their drinks there. My sister and I got government permits as "Exempt Persons" so we could drink, too. I still have the official certificate that says I'm exempt from the liquor laws because I am not Muslim.

Sometimes men from the bar would tell us places we should see on the island and how to get to them. We were even invited to the sultan's granddaughter's wedding—not the ceremony, but an enormous festive dinner afterward. The sultan was a lovely old man with a curly gray beard. He used to ride around town and smile and wave to people.

We stayed about a week before going back to the mainland.

We tried to climb Mount Kilimanjaro. We hired a guide and porters, bought supplies, and spent days, first climbing through tropical forest, then up over grassland and then bare stony land up to the saddle between the peaks. And then back down again—we weren't athletic enough or equipped to do the peaks. But I was probably the only soul who ever hiked up Kilimanjaro in a rayon dress and sneakers.

At the end, we went to Johannesburg to get a flight home. While we were there, we phoned Dr. Wulf Sachs to tell him how much we enjoyed reading his book *Black Anger*, about the African witch doctor he came to know as a patient and friend. He took us to meet the witch doctor, John Chavafambira, which was wonderful.

And then we went home.

And the musician? He married a girl who was also a musician, went on to teach at the Juilliard School of Music, and composed opera, ballet scores, piano and orchestral music, and jazz. He performed in a couple of concerts with Thelonious Monk. He died at 52 and had an obit in the *New York Times*.

OMOSHIROI NEE
(INTERESTING, ISN'T IT?)
by Mary Lee Maloney

In September of 1968, I found myself settling into the girls' dormitory of the Canadian Academy for my second year of high school in Kobe, Japan. My new roommate's name was Rebecca. We were given a dorm room along the hallway with a window facing out toward the side of Maya-san, the small mountain upon which the school stood. This view of the mountainside, though interesting from a geological and botanical point of view, was nothing like the view I had had the previous year when Ellen Marsh and I were at the far end of the hallway facing a penthouse view of the city of Kobe and the Sea of Japan.

I realized early on, Rebecca was a fascinating character to have as a roommate. She was obviously a bit eccentric, but that had never put me off about anybody. If she were a color, it would have been electric blue or bright turquoise. She had crystal blue eyes, an infectious smile, and a fringe of dyed marigold-blond hair circling her face like a monk's tonsure. She reminded me of one of those many-sided, colored origami paper boxes, chock full of interesting stories and insights into life.

An army brat, she had been all over the world and knew several languages. She sometimes talked in her sleep in German, Flemish or Japanese. This could be disconcerting, especially if she had taken any drugs prior to falling off to sleep. Sometimes she spoke several languages all within the space of one night. She had previously attended ASIJ, the American School in Japan, located in Tokyo, and spoke Japanese as it was spoken by native speakers, rather than the textbook Japanese I had learned.

Another intriguing thing about Rebecca was that she had a Japanese boyfriend, Isao. She had not only jumped the hoop linguistically into Japanese society, but had made the leap socially as well.

Rosemary had met Isao in Tokyo's trendy Shinjuku district and was pretty passionate about him, but realistic enough to know that nothing long term could come of this relationship. I have a photo, somewhere, of the two of them, which makes them resemble two peas in a pod, one with marigold hair cropped around her grinning face; the other with shiny black hair of about the same length around his handsome face.

What Rebecca gave me, which was invaluable, was a quick, bird's-eye view into the real Japan of that time. She told me stories about Shinjuku, the area of Tokyo where things were "happening." I got a feeling about how teens were thinking, the clothes they wore, and the causes for which they were demonstrating in the streets. I no longer felt as if I were looking at Japan through a glass darkly. It was as if Rebecca, with that crooked but infectious smile of hers, were pulling aside a curtain, saying, "Here it is, honey. Here is the real Japan."

Although we were the same age, Rebecca seemed eons older and more mature than I was. She "blew the portals of my mind" in a similar fashion as my stepfather, the psychoanalyst, had done. Here was a girl who had no compunction about stepping wholeheartedly into different cultures, a born extrovert. I was basically an introvert, but that didn't keep me from loving her down to the core of my being. She was a one-in-a-million individual, and I was blessed to have her as my roommate.

Penny, Rebecca, and I were a triumvirate. Threesomes are not supposed to work, but our bond was like a three-legged footstool. Penny had a raucous sense of humor that matched Rebecca's but with a decidedly more jaundiced view of things. She was Bob Dylan to Rebecca's John Lennon. Behind Penny's cobalt-blue eyes was the mind of a philosopher-queen and a bit of a sphinx. I called her Pegasus, not only because it was a play on her name but because there was something of the ages about her, as if she were mythically in tune with a certain wisdom from the past. Whereas Rebecca was a neon, electric advertisement for NOW, Penny was a thick leather-bound tome entitled, *Forever*.

Penny had an exotic beauty, a combination of Middle Eastern and Russian features. Her grandmother would not hear of Penny and me taking a trip home to the States following graduation. This was because the route home was to be via the Siberian Express. Even after many years in America, the family feared going anywhere near Russia. In later years, I read about the pogroms against the Jews and imagined what a struggle it must have been for Penny's grandmother and other family members to escape.

Once Penny gave me a pair of softly tooled leather sling-back heels, which she had purchased somewhere near Marrakech. These were the heels I was wearing when I made my swanfalls down the steepest portion of the hill at Canadian Academy. Rebecca, Penny, and I often walked down that hill on our way to downtown Kobe or to the shopping district of town, Sentagai. Another fall I took in those heels before giving up wearing them was down a flight of stairs at school. My boyfriend's good buddy, sociology teacher Barr Ashcraft, came along as I was sprawled out on the steps between the second and third floors of the high school's section of our school. Although I had given him the name of "the cynical pinnacle," Mr. Ashcraft seemed sincerely concerned about me. I had to stay there, sprawled out until the pain subsided and I could slowly unhinge myself from the hard stone steps.

Penny used to call me *yuwakai na nomi*, which meant "flirtatious flea" in Japanese. Why flea? Because I was 5 feet 7½ inches tall and weighed only about 120 pounds at the time. All legs and arms, I reminded Penny of a little flea with long appendages. Penny, Rebecca, and I thought this Japanese appellation for me was uproariously funny.

At that time, I still carried a torch for my boyfriend, Sam, who had gone off to Yale the previous year. I sent him a little ceramic fox about four inches high from the Japanese cemetery, Maya-san. Instead of enclosing a note, there was simply a familiar return address on the outside of the package. Within a couple of weeks, Sam and I were back in touch again, although 4,000 miles from each other.

Young people at this age remind me of thick sticks of colored chalk, the kind that street artists used for the beautiful renditions of classical paintings they drew on the pavements of Kobe. Evolving personalities, like soft pieces of chalk, keep their own basic color, but take on the hues of people with whom they come in contact, producing eclectic, multi-faceted images. Does this color go well with my own piece of chalk? Would it go even better with a dash of plum or a spray of cerise from the artist kneeling next to me? And so, the process of "becoming" continues.

What I remember of Rebecca and Penny are conversations we had and attitudes we shared. I can still remember Penny's laughter, a full-throated chortle with a little curl at the end. When Rebecca cracked up, she usually leaned back against the wall, if she were seated on her bed, and let out a staccato sound like a miniature jackhammer. So a little bit of Rebecca and Penny rubbed off onto me, and I'm sure a little bit of my personality rubbed off onto them. This, to my way of thinking, is not a negligible thing. Many years later, parts of different characters I have known are alive and well within me. Friends have become part of my spiritual DNA and I carry them around with me throughout my life. I'll trot out one of their phrases from time to time, and I know exactly to whom to attribute the words.

FISHING TRIP
by Deanne Thompson

When I was a young girl, my parents used to love to fish, or rather, my dad loved to fish. My dad had bought a little rowboat that he would hitch to the back of his car, pack his fishing gear and bait, worms Dad and I caught on the golf course the night before. With flashlight in hand I would help Dad pull the little wiggly night crawlers from the earth. Mom would find the shadiest spot, spread her blanket, and get one of her favorite books, a Perry Mason by Erle Stanley Gardner, a Pepsi, a sandwich, and her Pall Mall cigarettes. That was Mom's idea of going fishing.

There was another couple who were friends with my parents that also drove up to Wisconsin to fish. They had a daughter, Janet, who was a few years younger than I, but we were friends and always had fun. On the lakefront there was a large hotel and the two of us would go inside and play games or listen to the music. No television or hand-held video games, we had to use our imagination and entertain ourselves.

After a few years, the boat lost its appeal and became a pain in the neck to hitch up and pull around so it sat in the driveway. In the summer, my dad would ripen his tomatoes or any other vegetables from his garden in the boat. I remember the tomatoes because there were so many, and he would bag them up and take them around to friends and neighbors.

Last week I tried to find the place we went to in Wisconsin on a map. It was called Lake Ivanhoe, but it was nowhere to be found so I went on the Internet and it kept taking me to Lake Ivanhoe in Florida. I called Janet to see if she remembered anything about this place, but she couldn't find it either. I'm really curious to see if it exists anymore or if the name has changed. It was a beautiful place.

Recently, I heard from my granddaughter in Kenosha, Wisconsin. She and her husband and family knew exactly where this Lake Ivanhoe is. She has given me directions and a map, so I hope to visit there next summer if I am able.

MELALINDA
by Helen Levy

Robert Louis Stevenson's wife, Fanny, kept a diary from 1890 to 1893 when they lived in Samoa. It was published as a book titled *Our Samoan Adventure*. Twenty-two years before the Stevensons sailed to Samoa, Melalinda Leota Aiga, my great-grandmother, was born on Tutillulla, Pago Pago, Samoa. It is unlikely that the Stevensons and Melalinda ever met since she sailed out of the harbor of Pago Pago in 1881 to her new home in the Fiji Islands.

The tales of Melalinda's romance and life have been passed down the generations of my family. The handsome ship captain, William Wallace Wilson, was born in England in 1854 and immigrated as an infant with his parents and brother to New Zealand. William was not a cooperative student in school and at eighteen decided to run away with a friend to the Fiji Islands. He sailed the islands as a blackbirder, taking young and healthy natives to Australia to work in the cane fields.

The legend is that during his wandering, my great-grandfather met Melalinda on Tutillulla, Pago Pago, Samoa. Melalinda was a member of the chieftain family, and as a princess she was obliged to observe strict rules, interacting only with tribal family members. She was out-of-bounds to young sea captains.

William was permitted the favors of all the maidens on the islands except the royal ones, but he broke the rules and so did Melalinda. Here the facts get murky. William could not take her aboard without the whole tribe boarding his schooner. As he set sail for Fiji, some say he kidnapped her and others say she swam out to the ship, not necessarily out of love of William but because she was no longer a virgin and trouble was sure to follow. We will never know, but either way makes an interesting story.

William and Melalinda set up residence on top of the hill at Levuka, the capital of Fiji, and William was appointed Harbor Master by King Cakoban. Melalinda, who was also called Lizzie, was always the proud royal. She never deigned to master English, and William never bothered to learn Samoan. In any case, they managed to communicate often enough to produce six children, one of whom was my grandmother, Mary Wilson. They married finally, only to please their children when they were of marriageable age and suitors came courting. The six children were witnesses at their wedding.

In the only existing photo of Melalinda, she is dressed in European clothes and her hair is done up in the English style of that time. She looks solemnly into the lens and you would never suspect that she didn't even know the English word for camera.

AN AUSTRALIAN EXPERIENCE

by Pat Lee

Ron's doctorate in hand, we flew to Brisbane in mid-February with six-week-old Peter and Andy, our twenty-month-old firstborn. Ron had insisted on going back to his country to "serve the church," which he had already served in a tin-roofed shack in Tasmania and in Melbourne, where he had helped build a church. When we married, I told him that I would willingly go back to his country if he needed to do that. Now, with the position of deputy master of King's College in Brisbane awaiting us, we were on our way.

After many hours, the pilot said we'd have to land in Fiji because the Australian coast was fogged in. Some got off the plane to look around after we landed, but our family did not. Some very large, heavy-set men boarded the plane wearing headgear and longish skirt-like apparel. They carried machinery that shot volumes of mist, fumigating the plane and ourselves.

When we landed in Brisbane, we were greeted by rows of Quonset huts from World War II. I couldn't look at the sky. It was too bright, brighter than California, a scorching glare. King's College was in St. Lucia, a suburb of Brisbane and home to the University of Queensland. Next to it was the Presbyterian College, and down the road was the Women's College. Each college was run by a master, a deputy, and, in our case, a special lecturer who helped teach the twenty-five or so theological students preparing to become ordained ministers. They ranged from twenty-two to thirty-one in age and were an especially nice group of young men from all over Queensland. Student dormitories stretched out way beyond our house at one end of the campus. The lovely King's chapel stood midway, and the home of the lecturer was down by the river.

After the kids were put to bed, we collapsed on our bed, a large queen-sized standard issue in Australia. At its head was a frame holding mosquito netting. You pulled the net over the whole bed so it pooled on the floor. We pulled, pooled, and plunked ourselves down. The silence was broken by a high, piercing squawk cascading into hysterical laughter.

"What's that?" I asked.

"It's a kookaburra," Ron said.

"Oh God," I thought. "Where am I?"

Our house was new and large, with four bedrooms and a two-room bathroom, one for the toilet, the other for the tub and sink. The living room had a large fireplace with no blower so that in winter, when you stood in front of the fire warming yourself, your back was cold. Large sliding-glass doors at one end opened onto a concrete porch. The dining area at one end of the living room was near the kitchen. A long hall had bedrooms along the way. We had sold most of our possessions before leaving Evanston, keeping only two round, embossed brass plaques, two little antique chairs, my Spode dinnerware, and our sterling silver place settings. When these things arrived, only two Spode cups were broken. The house was furnished, but it was our treasures from home that made it ours.

Ivy geraniums grew all along one side of our house. Frangipanis bloomed on the grass beyond. Red-and-purple flowers blossomed on huge trees flanking the river, and in springtime Brisbane was a mass of flowers. The city prided itself on being a "city of bridges" although there were only three. Sprawling Brisbane: home to eight hundred thousand souls, Australia's third-largest city at that time, and one of the largest-landmass cities in the world.

We were in a new world. Brisbane was subtropical and hot. February was summer, and a two-and-a-half-year drought was going on. One evening on television news I saw a battered, brown rancher whose face was almost as deeply lined as the cracked earth on which he stood. Those earthen cracks looked more like crevasses. They were that broad and deep.

"It's been like this for seven years. I guess I'll have to give it up if it lasts much longer," he said.

I turned to Ron and said, "Seven years! What's that poor man going to do?"

The same broadcast noted wild camels were leaving the middle of the continent and rummaging whatever they could find from ranches in the outback. Camels? Australia? I was told that, yes, camels were out there. Long ago, perhaps, a wealthy Arab had bestowed gifts of camels on an Australian friend.

Early on, I marched down the hall to Peter's room as he lay napping. A large, shiny brown bug hugged the wall next to the Benjamin Bunny print I'd hung. What was it? "A flying cockroach," I was told. I didn't know cockroaches flew. But then I didn't know a lot of things. The mosquitoes, I knew, how they flew in at night and were really big. They pooled up by the ceilings and they would buzz, "Beesch, beesch." It was almost impossible to fall asleep even when only one of them kept you company under the mosquito netting. We had come from Chicago, with central heating and screens on our windows. Brisbane felt like Grand Rapids when I was growing up. I wrote to Mom and asked her for a case of Dove soap and could she please heave herself into a large crate and take the first plane to Brisbane?

Instead of Mom in a crate, I got a little camera. Ron gave it to me on Mother's Day to record our experience and send it home to Mom and Dad. But it was Ron's mom who came from Melbourne for an extended visit. I remember her standing in our dining alcove, looking at Andy and Peter for the first time. Her first words were, "The boys don't look anything like Ron." She made us rabbit stew. Eating rabbit meat was very common, and all the butchers carried it. Mum had a difficult life and, rather than make her feel bad at our good fortune, we hid the china purchases we'd made. She could never have afforded them.

That first or second week in Brisbane, I had to visit the U.S. Consulate downtown, a long trek from St. Lucia. I didn't understand why I had to go when I was still exhausted from the trip. Ron insisted he could not do it for me.

"Why?" I asked.

"They have to make sure I didn't bring some little black girl into the country," he answered. The White Australia policy was in full swing then. At that time I did not realize that many "white" Australians have Aboriginal blood flowing in their veins from a few generations back. Apparently they wished to deny that. Asian, Indian, and other darker-skinned students were welcome at universities, but government policy forced them to return home once their studies were completed.

"Mother, have you and your crate boarded that plane yet? Hurry! Hurry! I need a sounding board and a shoulder to weep on." Shortly after our arrival, I decided to cook oatmeal. As the brew boiled, I saw a gray-black film forming on top.

"What's that?" I asked.

"Oh those are weevils," Ron said.

"Weevils?"

"Yes, in this climate they easily infest bags of grain."

I dumped all of it down the drain. Later I learned to cook cereal and just let it be, maybe lightly skimming what I could off the top. No sense in dumping sustenance down the sink.

Though I shopped at Nifty Thrifty, a little grocery up the road from the college, a bread man and a meat man came regularly to the back gate. Early on, I bought a chicken and thought, "Surely this will taste like home." Well, not quite. The bird was tough. I could imagine its long skinny legs loping across a parched yard, carefree and quick. Nice for the chicken but sad for us. I guess you would call it free-range chicken. I never bought another from the meat man. Nifty Thrifty bought frozen-solid chickens from America.

The bread man and his wares were a different story. He immediately told me he liked "Yanks," that he had served in the war with Yanks in New Guinea. He remembered how big and efficient they were. They'd throw down an airfield in a few days and think nothing of it. They remember the Battle of the Coral Sea where American planes and ships stopped the Japanese from advancing on Australia. To this day, a special day is set aside when large American vessels steam into Sydney Harbor to mark this critical battle and to honor America's intervention. In fact, there is a spot above the city dedicated to the role American troops played at that critical time.

So much happened our first week or two in Brisbane that later Ron said he should have taken us to Melbourne instead, taking his chances on his home church conference rather than staying in the politically disruptive climate of King's College and the Queensland Methodist Conference. But we were weary and I had just given birth. Maybe the storm clouds would pass us by.

Even in our first week at King's, I noticed one young man after another trudging into Ron's office. It was discouraging, and Ron began to think about Melbourne. One day at lunchtime, I asked him, "Who are those boys and what do they want? I've seen so many of them trudging into your office."

"Those are theologies," Ron answered. "They want to resign, leave King's and the ministry. They're fed up with the situation at the college, its policies and structure."

There were many complaints, among them being they couldn't get married while training. The story goes that, long ago, the master and his wife had to wait seven years to marry. We were shocked. The boys were very frustrated and had dubbed King's master "God the Father" and Mr. B the gentle lecturer "God the Holy Spirit." Ron they called "God the Son," and you know what happened to him! Ultimately the boys stayed and so did we, for two years.

Ron's training and degrees brought us to King's. His faith and purpose and good heart kept us there. He made an impact in those two years, but we had to leave to save his professional growth and future. Ron had fine training in pastoral psychology, but the university's medical school did not hire him. When he applied for a position there they wanted someone with his skills, but we wondered whether they preferred Oxford or Cambridge graduates. We would have stayed in Australia if this job had been offered.

So once again we packed and left, hauling back our silver, dishes, and little antique chairs. Our psyches were battered, but our health was intact. We were starting over again, this time in a program at Menninger Clinic in Kansas. When Ron arrived in Topeka, he found an expected grant had been cancelled. As a result, he juggled two part-time jobs and his full-time Menninger program, and I was back to "making do," as they say in Australia, cooking gizzard stew for the family.

NEW YORK, NEW YORK
by Mary Lee Maloney

With all the blind optimism of youth, I set out for New York City following college. I headed for a place on West 13th Street in the Village. It was a Salvation Army house for working women called The Evangeline, just down the street from the Stanislavsky Acting School where Marlon Brando and so many other famous actors had studied.

My roommate and I shared a small room with brownish wallpaper, facing in the direction of Washington Square. She was an aspiring actress who worked as a waitress during the day. I remember thinking, "What a classic!" She was about my age, around twenty-one, chubby cheeked, with flowing brown curls, and popping blue eyes behind long lashes. She had this interesting way of always wearing hats, some of them even festooned with a feather or two.

"This is definitely a different kind of place than Boston," I thought to myself.

Early in the morning, before women of all ages headed down to the dining room of the Evangeline Inn for breakfast, there was the totally exotic "bathroom run." I say this factually and not at all in exaggeration. One had only to open the door of one's room, toothbrush in hand, heading down the hall to the communal bathroom, to be hit with a chorus of "New York, New York." These were not actresses or vaudeville hopefuls, but whole lines of pink-leotarded and tutu-skirted ballerinas slowly and methodically practicing their glissades and even grand jetés down the hallway in warm-up for early-morning classes at the New York City Ballet. Again, I was reminded of why my aspirations as a ballerina had been cut short at the age of seven.

These ethereal creatures, small-boned enough to fit three across, glided down the hallway, their hair tied up in identical topknots atop petite heads, eyes spotting straight ahead, no matter how quickly they spun around, and tiny elbows held up perpendicular to the carpet with hands draped slightly downward at the wrists. I could see how my large ankles and feet, even at a young age, had disqualified me from this parade of exquisite nymphs, looking as if they had stepped out of "A Midsummer Night's Dream." Ah, New York, I was coming under your spell, and I hadn't even been here a week.

My plan of action was to sign up for classes in sculpting at the Art Students League on 57th Street. I had had training working with clay with Lilly Swann Saarinen and had produced terra cotta sculptures such as the sculpture of my cat and the head of my dog, Jarl. Jarl won me honorable mention at the Cambridge Art Association across the Charles River from Boston. Here in New York, I had my eye on learning about subtractive sculpture in stone, where the idea was to chip off, with hammer and chisel, from the surface of a large block of stone until the desired effect was reached, and then spend hours polishing the stone.

But first, I had to land a job. The money my mother had kindly given me was running out. I spied something interesting in *The Village Voice*. A disabled woman needed help with her daughter, and with shopping and light housecleaning. I answered the ad. To my great surprise, this woman ended up being none other than the ex-wife of the famous Richard Leacock, the inventor of the light handheld 16-millimeter camera. This was the type of camera I had used at the University of Massachusetts to produce short films of my friends, complete with lap dissolves, where one scene fades into the next. I was in awe. A true case of serendipity. Before I knew it, I was walking Leacock's twelve-year-old daughter down to her private school, a few blocks away.

Mrs. Leacock, sadly, was totally bedridden at a fairly young age, due to having been on steroids too long for her rheumatoid arthritis. Her bones had sort of melted away. I had to sit her up in bed and literally do almost everything for her. She had a certified nursing assistant, CNA, as well, to help her with the bathroom and bathing. I did her housework and shopping. This was pleasant work for me simply because, in a sense, I felt honored to be helping this famous man's ex-wife, and she and I had interesting conversations about filmmaking.

One day the city's darker side confronted me. I had arrived at the Leacock condo at about 7:30 one morning. I helped Victoria get her breakfast fixed and assisted her in getting ready for school. Victoria and I said good-bye to her mother and headed for the elevator. On the way out of the building, I noticed an ambulance and several police cars parked in front. I wondered what was up, as did Victoria. Then I heard a voice say the word "suicide." Quickly I put my hand alongside Victoria's face, the side closest to the ambulance, and rushed her from the scene. We saw nothing.

My work at Leacock's only lasted a few weeks. There was some altercation with a Jamaican CNA who claimed she wasn't getting the agreed-on rate. It had nothing to do with me, but I witnessed this irate and very strong woman stand at the foot of Mrs. Leacock's bed and bounce her bed up and down a few times. This was a pretty untoward scene, and I didn't know what to make of the whole event. I just remember admiring the strong cadence of the Jamaican woman's voice as she made her case with Mrs. Leacock. Because I neglected to call the police, Mrs. Leacock let me go.

Before I knew it, I was working at the Barbizon Hotel on Fifth Avenue, a famous women's hotel and residence. I worked as a room service waitress, taking orders and delivering trays of food for breakfast and lunch. This was sort of demeaning work for a college graduate, but I had no qualms about it. The jobs I looked for in New York were, in my mind, simply a means toward an end. I needed to make enough money to survive in the city while I took sculpting classes at the Art Students League.

The Barbizon Hotel turned out to be somewhat seamy, with many young women looking and sounding as if they were right out of *The Valley of the Dolls*. To my knowledge, I didn't think I was actually dealing with anyone on hard drugs or illicit drugs such as heroin, but I did get the impression that there was a lot of pill popping at the Barbizon. I remember one young woman in particular. Her blond hair was falling over her face, and she almost stumbled at the doorway as I handed her tray to her. She was so obviously on something, and not that much older than I was. It was all I could do to keep myself from saying something that would have been caring though inappropriate. I couldn't understand why people would do this to themselves. There was just so much that was a mystery to me in those days when I felt like a debutante coming out in the world. Ah, New York, New York.

FIRE!
by Beata Hayton

After my return from Africa, some friends introduced me to Bill Hayton, a University of Chicago law graduate who was bright and kind and fun. We got married on St. Patrick's Day, which was Bill's birthday—so he could remember the date, and my little nephews sang at our wedding, which was wonderful.

Bill and I loved to travel. We covered a lot of ground—England, France, Russia, Switzerland, Greece, Egypt, Morocco, China, Japan. I can't remember them all. It wasn't always easy, though. The night our hotel caught fire, for instance.

It was the end of a trip to Egypt, and we were staying in a big hotel near the airport because we were flying home the next day. It was a nice modern hotel. The lobby was a big airy space, open all the way to the top of the building, and the restaurant and bar had handsome wall hangings with Egyptian motifs.

We had a pleasant dinner and went to bed, but in the middle of the night I woke up, smelling smoke. I woke Bill and went to the window. Down at ground level I could see flames. I picked up the phone and the operator said, yes, madam, there is a problem and we should take the stairs down. I don't know why they didn't sound an alarm for everybody. Anyways, we pulled on the clothes we had laid out and I soaked a couple towels in the washbasin. We felt the door, opened it cautiously, and started down the stairs holding the wet towels over our faces to keep from breathing in the smoke, and held onto the railings to guide ourselves down. It was six flights down to the bottom.

At one point, I remember, there was someone lying on the stairs. I don't know if he or she was dead or alive, and I'm sorry to say we were too upset and anxious to stop and see. When we reached the bottom, there were other hotel guests outside, and hotel employees brought us blankets for warmth because the night air was cool. Eventually, we were taken to another big hotel where we could sit in the lobby and be warm. The next day, the consulate gave us new passports and got us on a plane home. We got most of our luggage back, although the souvenirs I had bought had disappeared from my bag.

Seventeen people died that night, we learned later, probably from smoke inhalation. What caused the fire? They were serving a fancy flaming dish for supper; apparently the draperies in the dining room caught fire, and then someone opened the windows and the flames spread out into the lobby. The smoke rose up through every floor.

One thing I remembered after that was to keep important items, like a passport, close at hand when we went to bed. The other was to check the stairs when we moved into a hotel. And one hotel, in China, I think, was using the back stairs to store old furniture.

KIM
by Diane Ciral

Our home is near the end of the block facing Lake Michigan, part of a development of twenty-six houses on Castlewood Terrace, built on Lake Michigan landfill in the 1930s, before Lake Shore Drive, Marine Drive, and Lincoln Park were conceived. The two corner lots, one on our side, the other, across the street, remained vacant for many years because of a covenant that ruled for only detached single-family residences. In the early 1970s, a group of city farmers organized by the University of Illinois Extension Service tried growing vegetables in these two sandy and rocky lots. None had succeeded until the Korean farmers came.

There is a scrape, scrape sound from outside, then wheels slowly moving, then silence. I look at the clock. It is 3:30 in the morning. The windows of our bedroom are wide open. I fall back to sleep, but the same noise awakens me again. This goes on for quite some time before I sleepily drag myself out of bed to look out the window. There, down below in the early-morning light, I see an old man using a bucket to scrape water out of the gutter, leftover water from the sprinkling system across the street. I stand there for quite some time watching the old gentleman scrape up the water into his bucket, put it into his shopping cart, wheel it to the empty lot that abuts our yard, and repeat the process all over again.

I dress quickly and go downstairs. The old man is digging in the sandy, rocky earth. He speaks no English and I speak no Korean, but somehow I convince him to come into my garden where I show him the long, green water hose. I pull it across the expanse of lawn to reach through the fence. I turn on the water.

A big grin, showing a missing side tooth, spreads across his face as he realizes that he can use my water to grow his plants. I give him a piece of paper with my name and phone number on which I have written a brief note saying that he can come to my garden any time for water. That evening I receive a call from his grandson, thanking me. He tells me that the old man's name is Kim. He lives on Clarendon and Montrose, not far from us.

Soon, I begin finding strange-looking vegetables at my front door, bok choy, snow peas, and other vegetables whose names I do not know. Kim is sharing part of his crop with me. I call his grandson and ask if Kim would be available for weeding my garden. I say that I would pay his grandfather for a few hours of work a week. Kim refuses to take the money but returns each week to do my weeding.

Just before Christmas that year, I bring Kim a gift of a warm goose-down jacket from Eddie Bauer. Initially, he refuses it but eventually I convince him to accept it.

The gardens are gone now, replaced by seven single-family detached homes. The Korean gardeners have been dispersed to other empty lots in the community; none of their gardens so fine and neat as the rows of vegetables that grew next door during those summers long past.

For a few winters, I see Kim pedaling his bike down Sheridan Road, huddled in his down jacket. At each sighting, I remember his green vegetable garden beyond my fence.

A CLOSE CALL
by Mary Lee Maloney

Whenever I'm in danger, I think of this experience, and the perspective it gives makes me feel lucky. One day, not too many days away from the time I left San Francisco to find an apartment across the bay in Berkeley, I went down to Chinatown for a stroll in the waning sunlight. After about an hour of window shopping and hunting through well-known shops for odds and ends, such as the black cotton Mary Jane shoes that I ran around in back then, I headed toward a brand new McDonald's, which had just gone in on Chinatown's Grant Street. What was Ronald McDonald doing among rare ceramic peach decorations, jade bangles, cinnabar bangles and necklaces, and onyx rings glittering behind the age-old dust-encrusted windows of San Francisco's Chinatown?

Anything for the tourists, I suppose. You could tell that many of the Chinese-American women working in Chinatown shops would just as soon never see another troublesome tourist again. I used to feel sympathetic towards them when they would give me a hardened tone of voice and rush me along. I knew that hordes of people from all over the country and the world had maybe made them a small fortune, but that these women probably would prefer a small shop, no doubt, with fewer intruders from outside of the neighborhood.

As I sat munching my fish sandwich in the new McDonald's, I was surprised to see that quite a few Chinese Americans were also curious about the new fast-food place on the block and were chasing down their sandwiches with Sprite along with me. A Chinese-American man, stocky and affable, sat facing me where he had moved in, about a table away. His dark eyes smiled at me in a familiar way as he asked how often I came this way, through Chinatown. I told him I was a great fan of Chinatown and probably ended up here once every other week.

I was surprised that this man seemed to want to talk with me as much as he did. I welcomed conversation with him, since most Chinese seemed somewhat diffident. Unless I was in Chinatown with friends, I usually chatted with no one and kept my own company.

After going on about several topics, in a small-talk kind of way, he asked me if I would like to take a ride with him in his red Ferrari. He seemed to be in his mid-thirties and was certainly an interesting conversationalist. I saw no problem in taking a spin around town with this friendly character, so I quickly accepted the invitation. Soon Kirk, as he was called, had pulled out from the streets of Chinatown and we were headed down Mission Street toward Van Ness Boulevard, where my friend Juana and I had watched many an exhilarating Gay Rights Parade in fascination. Passing Van Ness, we whizzed by other areas familiar to me from many bus trips down to Ocean Beach to watch the Pacific Ocean and to pick up a fine mist of salt upon my face.

Suddenly, Kirk was veering the car off towards a relatively unpopulated area called the Presidio. This area, I knew, used to be a naval station during World War II. It sported wide expanses of concrete and looked, at that time, like a huge parking lot. No one was in sight. I knew, at once, that I should not have gone on this ride. What had I been thinking?

It was a repeat of the time I had insisted with my mother that my kind-hearted neighbor on the first floor of the Victorian house where I lived in Cambridge, Massachusetts, had no ulterior motives when he wanted to cook dinner for me. My mother had insisted otherwise, and it turned out she was right. I just hadn't wanted to think that a man could act in such an ungentlemanly fashion.

But the stakes, here, were slightly higher. Things were not looking good at all. If I wanted to keep myself from becoming a statistic, I had better start thinking pretty fast.

I remember invoking the spirit of my wise stepfather, Dr. James Clark Moloney, the psychoanalyst my mother had married and divorced a few years back. Clark would know how to psych this guy out. What would he say to do in a situation such as this one? In all his years of dealing with psychopaths and others, what words of wisdom would he have for me?

All of a sudden, Kirk brought the car to a stop in the middle of the Presidio, and took the keys out of the ignition. Then he grabbed my left wrist, roughly. My wrist was small, at the time, and Kirk's hand easily encircled it in a meaty grasp. Instinctively, I knew that, if I reacted in any way, it would be, as in a chess game, Kirk's move next. If, on the other hand, I refused to acknowledge what my senses told me, then I would also deny Kirk his chance, psychologically, for a next move.

I don't know if my stepfather, Clark, actually was helping me out, but I had a strong conviction that, whatever I did, I must not let this guy know that I was nervous about his grasping my wrist, and I must not let him see my fear. If I did, I sensed it would be all over. I could end up raped, beaten up, or even killed. I could hear the water from the bay lapping nearby.

As these dire thoughts raced through my head, I bestowed myself an Academy Award for my acting. I pretended I was on the telephone back in Orchard Lake, Michigan, during junior high school. What was it Sue and I were talking about so amiably? Was it the latest antic of her pet Chihuahua or was it the best color of Slicker lipstick to wear to the Sadie Hawkins dance? The idea was to keep up a light banter, involving Kirk in thoughts divergent enough to entertain him, take his mind off of his own preoccupations, and totally change the mood on him. I also thought that, if I could do this effectively enough and for long enough, I might bore him to death, and he would think better of his plans.

At one point, my resolve began to slip. When I could see that my stories, so far, had not caused Kirk to loosen his grasp, a part of me felt like breathing heavily and screaming out the fear that I naturally felt. But I had a very good imagination. I realized that, the minute I stopped seeing my companion as the friendly conversationalist I had first thought him to be, then I was, in effect, acknowledging that he had broken a sort of social contract, and I was forcing his hand to do what—grasp my wrist tighter and with his other hand cover my mouth and nose? This would surely cause me to gasp and sputter and scream in alarm. The jig would be up, at that point. It would be almost impossible to get either one of us calmed down again and thinking rationally enough to stop the expected outcome of such a scene.

I waxed on, for the life of me, about something I found to be somewhat amusing. Maybe, at this point, I was telling Kirk, in tones of intimacy, what a special time it had been when friend Ghita's older brother had driven his Mercedes-Benz down to the city to give her and her friends from the Mary Elizabeth Inn a ride down to Carmel, in honor of Ghita's twenty-first birthday. How blue the ocean was as we sped along the narrow road! Stevie Wonder was singing on the tape deck, "Isn't She Lovely?" Juana, Wendy, and I were in the back seat; Ghita and her handsome subcontinent Indian brother were sitting up front. The fresh ocean breeze in our hair, as we whizzed along in the Mercedes, felt so delectable, it almost seemed to have a flavor.

Perhaps I continued with an amusing story I had about a man I thought looked a lot like a young version of Clark Gable—my, he was handsome! This, to the extent that Juana and others showed up in the drawing room at the Mary Elizabeth Inn, purposely, to get a glimpse of him when he showed up to take me out. I could tell that Juana figured that I may have, somehow, located the one true male specimen in the city of San Francisco, other than her own boyfriend.

But, as it turned out, wouldn't you know, once I got into the car with this Clark Gable look-alike, he started going strange on me. One stoplight he would affectionately cup my right shoulder in his hand. The next stoplight, as he cruised the car to a smooth stop, his wrist, literally in the air, his fingers waving around, like squid, giving a new meaning to the expression, "limp-wristed." *Quel* disappointment!

No, actually, I don't think I would have launched into that story with Kirk. But you get the idea. The tone was more important than almost anything I said. It was to be totally unconcerned, convivial, and intriguing. The mind was to be totally safe from realizing that, as the minutes ticked by, Kirk's grasp was becoming sweaty, my sequestered wrist, more and more painful. Kirk's eyes looked tense. I tried not to look at them. I mostly gazed out the window at the coming dusk over the Presidio. It now had to be about 5:30 on a fall day. I could tell that Kirk did not really want to do this. Little beads of perspiration sprung up along his businessman's upper lip. Maybe, in some sick sense, he felt it was expected of him to try this with any woman dumb enough to get into his car. I would just prove his expectations wrong.

My stepfather, Clark, was proud of me, I could feel. He applauded my ability to see this character as the hurting, bewildered man that he was. Maybe it had helped me, many years ago, when, as a twelve-year-old, I had carefully inspected pen-and-ink drawings an artist had made for Clark's book, *Fear: Contagion and Conquest*. I had looked these pictures over, not only for their artistic style, but also for their possible meaning.

When I imagined a little boy curled up as if he were still in his mother's womb within the menacing form of the policeman wielding his stick, I learned a lesson on a visceral level. Many men may be hiding a vulnerable and totally hurt child within the uniform of the soldier, the policeman, the violent offender. The rage, the anger, the offensive action hide the raw wound of never feeling they were enough, of never having been protected and loved as children.

After probably close to an hour at the Presidio, Kirk finally let go of my wrist. I could feel his relief, as well as my own. He told me that the Chinese had been so discriminated against in this city that he had just wanted to hurt someone who was white.

Just as with everything else that evening, I acknowledged nothing. I acted as if I hadn't heard his explanation. Part of me feared coming out of my self-imposed trance to recognize reality. What if the spell broke and he attacked me at this point? No, best to keep up the façade, acting like a little "witless wonder" until Kirk finally dropped me off, unharmed, in front of the Mary Elizabeth Inn, on

Bush Street, in San Francisco. This, eventually, unbelievably, he did do. My would-be rapist turned back into a real gentleman at the end of the evening, after all. I had refused to treat him as anything but his gentlemanly self, and, miraculously, he had returned to that image of himself.

THANKSGIVING
by Diane Ciral

Thanksgiving is my favorite holiday. It's like a Norman Rockwell painting, our family table lovingly crowded with grandparents, children and grandchildren, aunts and uncles, all admiring the crisply golden turkey. November 1976, our guest list was even longer. Our family Thanksgiving was seen on national television.

July 4th of that same year, I took my fifteen-year-old daughter Jody with me to visit the Vietnamese refugee camp at Fort Indiantown Gap, Pennsylvania. My brother Dick, who was the director of Region Five, U.S. Health and Human Services, during the Ford administration, had been appointed to resettle 35,000 Vietnamese refugees in America.

I was a social activist working on many committees from the arts to urban planning. I saw a need to help the poor in my own Uptown community and couldn't understand why we were bringing Vietnamese refugees to the United States when there was such a great need here at home. I had come to Fort Indiantown Gap as a doubter and came away a believer. Never had I met people as gentle and kind, as dedicated to democracy, as willing to learn and work and become productive citizens. It was then that I told Dick, after conferring with my husband, Shev, that we would be willing to sponsor a Vietnamese family in Chicago. Not only did we help to settle the eight people in our own family and the sixteen in Dick's family, but Dick thought of a group sponsorship committee to bring in more refugees and share responsibilities.

A few weeks before Thanksgiving of that year, Dick and I bought turkeys and all the trimmings and delivered them to each of the Vietnamese families. Late in the afternoon, the day before Thanksgiving, ABC television contacted Dick about doing a lead story on the Vietnamese refugees' first Thanksgiving in America. Dick and I decided that the refugee families we had sponsored should celebrate Thanksgiving at our house all together.

Since it was too late to find turkeys that weren't frozen, we contacted each of the families and brought their turkeys to our house. Preparing for an additional thirty guests for the following day called for great organization. Tables and chairs were brought up from the basement, dishes came down from shelves, tablecloths and napkins were ironed. Our house was a beehive of activity, with everyone pitching in. Well, almost everyone.

I awoke at 4:30 in the morning Thanksgiving Day to start putting turkeys in the oven, making dressing, sweet potatoes, cranberries, and vegetables nonstop. Shev was nowhere to be seen. When the doorbell rang that afternoon with the ABC-TV camera crew, he emerged from the basement where he had disappeared all day, completely unaware of the frenetic preparations going on upstairs. The crew filmed the arrival of our Vietnamese families as well as their children throwing snowballs in the backyard. It was the first time the families had ever seen snow.

At 6 p.m., we gathered in front of the television set, waiting to be seen and heard on the news. The cameras captured the snowball throwing, the gathering of Americans and Vietnamese to give thanks on this special holiday and, last, the reporter asked what this holiday meant to us, as sponsors. The interview that was shown on the news wasn't with Jorie, who was noon anchor on NBC news, nor was it Dick, who had spent months coordinating the Vietnamese refugee resettlement program, and it wasn't with me. It was my darling husband who gave the most beautiful and caring thoughts about how we, as Americans, were sharing this special day with refugees who had come to this country with hope for a better future.

The last shot of the Thanksgiving story on national television was of my backside and my hands covered with oven mitts lifting the last turkeys out of the oven.

FINISHING NYANSHA
by Sarah Mirkin

We're careening down a road. It's a road that is unpaved, rutted from drought, made unbearable by the lack of shock absorbers in the Land Rover, which is kicking off clouds of red dust that obscure visibility. We're driving the 96 kilometers from Kigoma to Kasulu in western Tanzania, where the road takes us as close to Nyansha as we can get by car.

It's early October 2009, but I can't tell you what day it is. The day doesn't matter. What does matter is the intense heat and the dust, which penetrate the closed, air-conditioned car. Between the north-bound road, which we are on, and the southbound road is a construction site. It is a road the World Bank is building between Kigoma and Kasulu. Stretches of it are already paved and, when we can focus and despite the bone-jarring jolts, we look longingly at the paved stretches. We realize we are not on a road at all but on a kind of side strip made passable only by the vehicles that have preceded us.

"We" is part of our little safari group: my son and daughter-in-law, my daughter, our guide Joseph Kitia, and our driver. We have great confidence in Mr. Kitia. He has been my guide on all four safaris to Tanzania. He is president of his village, Usa River, on the eastern side of the country. I have entrusted him with me and my family even though he is not familiar with this area of his country. Our driver is a burly Tanzanian, a Muslim named Mohammed. Joseph has hired him because his price was "reasonable." The project director, Jackson, whom we will meet in Kasulu this evening, would have charged us twice as much for another driver, or so Joseph tells us. The quality of the drivers in Tanzania is in direct correlation to their cost. Mohammed is driving like a madman, probably about 60 mph. He seems to delight in passing cars when there is something directly in front of the vehicle we are passing. When we gasp at the near miss, he beams at us.

Joseph pleads, "Mohammed, slow down! We have a whole family here." The plea goes unheeded. Mohammed will risk lives no matter the nature of the cargo.

The trip takes about two hours. As the engine heats up, it overcomes the cooling effect of the air conditioning until the air in the car is clogged with moist, red dust. My daughter, a veteran traveler, finally yells out, "Open the window! We are suffocating in here!" We finish the trip in the heat of the late afternoon, limp, damp, and exhausted.

As we whiz past an old truck carrying a lot of baskets, I reflect on the very possible crash that could take all our lives. It comes to me very clearly that, if I survive this trip, I should try to record it. More than ever, I see the necessity of completing and recording this project my husband, Dr. Bernard L. Mirkin, was not able to finish. His abrupt death in August 2007 ended his work in Nyansha long before it was completed.

Our mission to the remote village of Nyansha is to visit the health clinic Bernard had been building over the past eight years to provide health care to the villagers who often cannot make the trip to the hospital in Kasulu, a distance of five kilometers. The health clinic, when completed, would be the first health care offered to the ten thousand villagers of Nyansha.

Bernard started this project in 2000 after meeting Mbiha Jackson Kabona, a professional safari guide, on our first safari to Tanzania in 2000. He and Jackson had had long conversations during that trip in which Jackson told Bernard of the serious plight of the population in his native village of Nyansha. Although Jackson's information about the village concerned the incidence of HIV/AIDS, Bernard discovered over the ensuing years that AIDS was only one of a number of serious diseases in Nyansha, none of which was being diagnosed or treated. But it was Jackson's emphasizing that half of his graduating class had already died of AIDS that hit Bernard at the center of his physician's soul. He had taken an oath to heal the sick, and here was a challenge that surmounted any other he had encountered.

After long efforts to raise funds for this health clinic and end-less e-mails to and from Jackson, Bernard made a trip to Nyansha in October of 2004. He wanted to see where the health clinic would be, meet the village elders, and interview some of the villagers about their expectations of the clinic. He took with him his friend John Buenz, architect for the entire project, and George Schau, who had experience building housing in South Africa for Habitat for Human-ity. Bernard, John, and George stayed three days in Nyansha, during which they were hosted by Jackson, who was acting as the project director for the Nyansha "Circle of Life."

During their visit, the three men stayed in a new motel on the outskirts of Kasulu, the first motel in Kasulu. It was hoped that it would attract tourists. They were the first guests in the motel. In the rooms, sinks were in place and water was available, but there were no connections between the water and the sinks. The men had to bring water into the rooms, pour the water into the sinks, which had been stopped up with rags, wash, then pull the rags out of the drains to let the water run out onto the floor, since no pipes connected the sinks with a drainage system. New beds were covered with clean linens but the floors had not been swept, so there were dead bugs awash in the water draining from the sink. Clothes could be draped over the chair or hung on a few hooks. One light bulb illuminated each small room. Bernard remarked that it was just as well since he did not want to scrutinize his surroundings.

The afternoon following their arrival, Jackson accompanied the three men to the site of the clinic for a welcome ceremony. About a hundred people attended the ceremony to witness Bernard being inducted into the Ha tribe. He sat on a small stool about seven inches off the ground, no small feat for a seventy-five-year-old man, who was 6 feet 2 inches tall. The elders placed a warrior garment on him made from tree bark, and he was given a spear, an axe, and a sheathed knife. This was followed by incantations from the elders.

Five years later, I was also given a welcome ceremony but was made a member of the woman's club. There was no Ha tribe membership for me, even though by that time we had actually raised enough money to finish the clinic. Instead of a spear, axe, and knife, I was given two hand-woven baskets. Hunting and gathering were clearly gender-oriented.

Jackson was waiting for us when we arrived in Kasulu five years after Bernard's visit. He was not pleased with our choice of Joseph as guide, since it was clear that Jackson considered the Nyansha project his and would make every effort to control the visit as much as possible. Although about eight more rooms had been added to the motel, conditions had not changed much. They had only multiplied. The one light bulb remained, the drainage pipes had been connected, and water did actually flow from faucets into the sink. There was a small television set on an old table in each room, but these did not work. We had our laundry done, which was returned to us at the end of the day, folded but still wet. The day we arrived, our beds were made but, in the four days and three nights we stayed in the motel, the beds were never made up.

Jackson met us that night at the restaurant outside of the motel. He arrived on a handsome motorbike with a back seat, which was occupied by his older brother, Fanuel, a preacher in the village of Nyansha. I had been waiting to see that motorbike. Some months earlier, I had wired money to Jackson for its purchase. It was to be used by the clinic's medical director for transportation to the Nyansha clinic, since there were no suitable lodgings for him in the village. A week or so after wiring the money, I got an e-mail from Jackson telling me that he had had an accident with his new motorbike and was injured. Could I help him pay his medical bills? That was how I discovered that he had purchased the bike for himself. He kept it in Nyansha at his brother's house when he worked in Arusha, which was on the other side of the country.

I had not seen Jackson in nine years, and my memory of his appearance was dim since I had not interacted with him as closely as Bernard had. He had aged considerably, not surprising since he suffered from both diabetes and malaria, a common predicament among

Tanzanians. He and Fanuel stood alongside our dining table, waiting to be asked to sit down, and refusing food when it was offered. Jackson was obviously nervous. He had our visit planned out using the $500 I had sent him to arrange meetings for us and, he said, to open bank accounts for the prospective clinic staff the next morning.

As I listened to Jackson, I could feel the anger rising in me. Here I was, halfway around the world, below the equator, and I was getting angry at this gaunt forty-five-year-old man as he laid out what he had arranged for us in an attempt to reassert himself as leader of this project, not with Dr. Mirkin, but with Mama Sarah. The immediate cause of my anger was the result of a very recent event that had altered the reason for our trip. In late July 2009, I had wired $3,000 to Jackson to buy the drugs necessary for the clinic's dispensary and to pay three-months' salary for each of three workers so that the clinic could open. Our original plan was to travel to Nyansha in October to see the clinic in its early stage of operation. In August, I received a cryptic e-mail from Joseph Kitia, our guide, reporting that he had contacted Jackson to confirm some arrangements for the trip and was told that there was no money.

I e-mailed Jackson, copying Joseph, to ask what had happened to the funds. Several days passed. Then Jackson wrote to say that, as he was traveling from the bank in Dar es Salaam to the medical supplies company where he was to buy the drugs for the clinic, he was robbed of the $10,000 he was carrying. He said he had been too upset to tell me and had been hospitalized for injuries. This was all the money left in the Mirkin Memorial Fund and, in Tanzania, a huge sum. For comparison, the annual salary for the chief medical officer at the clinic is $7,700. So Jackson had supposedly lost a year's wages and then some. The mission of our trip was converted into an effort to assess the overall situation in Nyansha, to deal with Jackson, and to attempt to set up a better arrangement for operating the clinic.

Only Jackson's words in an e-mail sent on August 19, 2009 can capture the nature of his event. "Dear Mama Sarah, I am very sorry for not writing for since I arrived in Arusha for thorough medical check-up,

I think some few questions were answered by Joseph concerning our work in Nyansha. I did not write to you for those days because I got a very bad event which will put me into trouble with you if I will not get the solution soon before your arrival. On the day I withdrawn the fund for purchasing drugs I robbered by the bandits when entering into the taxi going to the medical store for purchasing. I was badly affected and admitted to the clinic for those days and I did not have any words to explain what happened, instead I was going here and there to my friends and relatives to help me get money for at least purchase the drugs and the clinic start operate before your arrival. This is very bad to me, and I have tried so far and nothing have been obtained though I am still working hard to make sure we operate before your arrival."

"This is bad news indeed," I replied. "I am sorry that this has happened, and we will have to think about how this affects our project in Nyansha. As I told you before I left Chicago, the funds I sent you for salaries and drugs was the last money in the Bernard Mirkin Memorial Account. I will not have time to raise more funds before I leave for Tanzania. It is VERY important that something is operating at the Nyansha clinic when I arrive there."

Jackson replied, "I am working hard to finding replacement so that I maintain our work as per our plans. I am expecting to have a support from my relatives as I have involved them so that we find a solution in order to keep our spirit on this project high. I do not want to miss this relationship as to understand this event is quite hard and the police is still working on it. To sell a motor bike will be possible but will take time because in the village is very hard to have someone who can buy it, but will try to find one when I get there. I am still in Arusha and this event have contributed to develop low blood pressure. I am getting medication so that I make my sugar and this blood pressure into normal or better for me to travel back to the village before your arrival. If I get $3,876 will be enough for me to purchase enough drugs to open the clinic."

About three weeks later, when I was making last arrangements for the trip to Tanzania, I heard again from Jackson. "Mama Sarah,

I have received your e-mail and it is very sad to inform you that I have not yet found any replacement of the fund stolen. Due to this problem I therefore want to tell you that on your visit in Nyansha you may find operations going on or not. But my hope is operations to be on during your visit. I cannot say anything now as I am still in Arusha where I can find a solution of this problem. Asante for now, Sincerely, Jackson."

My anger went deeper than that event. Bernard had spent seven years working with Jackson to develop the Nyansha Circle of Life Project. Perhaps my growing anger was the recognition of the brutal contrast between what Bernard had accomplished over seven years and how little help he had received from either the U.S. or Tanzania. On this side, architect John Buenz had developed an elegant set of plans for village services on a nineteen-acre plot of land sold to the Nyansha project from the village. The four buildings included the health clinic, a pre-school, a women's small business center, and a community meeting place. Bernard had raised $104,425 in the seven years, mostly from friends and colleagues and one foundation. His files were packed with proposals to national and local foundations asking for support of his efforts. Most of his requests were declined. According to most institutional funders, a small, remote project could not be evaluated sufficiently to justify even a small investment. His physician friends, whom he hoped to include in a group practice of traveling doctors, were either too old and infirm to commit to the risks of working in Nyansha, or they felt that Nyansha was not "developed sufficiently" to warrant their carrying on research projects that might enhance their status in their respective academic departments.

Human need was only of marginal interest, Bernard discovered. But he soldiered on. He found some diagnostic kits at a local laboratory and was assembling supplies of drugs for the clinic's dispensary, even though the building was far from complete. He continued his correspondence with Jackson, encouraging him to believe in the project and to keep developing it despite the slow progress. The Tanzanian side was not delivering much either. The land was available, but there was no one in the village, besides Jackson, who stepped up to offer help. The Tanzanian Ministry of Health offered letters of encouragement but kept silent about any commitment of funds or labor.

Bernard's passion was to heal the sick. As he developed this project in the several years before his death, he inserted it into every conversation he could, often when it related to nothing that was being discussed. Many a guest at a dinner party or at a restaurant was subjected to a long narration of the plight of the villagers in Nyansha, how the project was faring, and then the expectation that the unwilling listener would adorn Bernard with admiration for something only he could carry out. I came to understand that he was trying to talk himself into continuing the project when he knew there was so much against it. What had kept him going for nearly seven years with only one dejected African to help him? In all that time, he and Jackson had some kind of strange understanding that they would do this alone.

WEAVING THE
THREADS

SCRUBBING CARROTS ON SUNDAY MORNING
by Penelope Whiteside

Today I am at the kitchen sink, patiently scrubbing five pounds of carrots. I shall be cutting them into little coin-shaped pieces soon enough. This is because I'm bringing the tzimmis to the Passover celebration on Monday. It is Palm Sunday. The day is bright with the promise of spring. I'm thinking about not going to the church service this morning.

As I scrub the carrots, I remember Palm Sundays when I was young. We waved the palms that they gave us, marched down the block when the weather was mild, or inside the church itself when winter still lingered. We sang "Hosanna" in imitation of those who welcomed Jesus to Jerusalem, imagining how His followers spread their palms before the donkey Jesus rode through the gate of that holy city to celebrate Passover. We were almost giddy with borrowed ecclesiastical happiness! Perhaps it was a sunny spring day much like this one.

Palm Sunday lost its joy a few years back, though. Yes, we still receive palms, but our hosannas are burdened by the somber business we know lies ahead. Nowadays, Palm Sunday services are chiefly about the trials that led to Jesus's crucifixion. There are reenactments of the trials, first before the high priests, then before Pilate, the Roman administrator. Different members of the congregation take the parts of Herod, Pilate, and even Jesus. We, the ones sitting in the pews, rise to our feet on cue to shout, "Crucify him, crucify him!"

I have finished cutting the carrots, dumping the rough ends of them into the bright-red garbage can that slides out from under the sink.

It's not that I don't get the point of this newer version of Palm Sunday. We are supposed to remember that it was our sins that nailed

Jesus to the cross. In the old days, I confess that it was all too easy to think of the crucifixion as a long-ago event, a bump on the happy road to Easter. We were the scot-free benefactors who, of course, had nothing to do with that piece of ancient history.

One of my Catholic friends was taught when she was little that her sins reopened the wounds of Jesus. Similarly, this current Palm Sunday is supposed to remind us that we are not off the hook after all. As I admire the carrots, those firm bright coins I have created, the start of the 10:30 service draws closer and closer. I shall parboil the carrots in my large red pot.

I wonder what Jesus ate for Passover, that last supper before the Cross. Was there tzimmis back then? Did they even have carrots and sweet potatoes in the Holy Land? All that we Christians ever hear about are the bread and the wine, also the foot washing, Jesus cleaning the dusty feet of his disciples before the meal began. The carrots have not begun to soften yet. The sweet potatoes, five pounds at the store scale, seem to have shriveled a little since I baked them in their skins last night. I'm hoping the carrots don't overwhelm them. Abby, the friend who has invited us to Passover, is expecting thirty.

It is five minutes before the church service is to begin. I had better check the carrots. They are done now. I peel the skin off the sweet potatoes. My old recipe for making tzimmis calls for honey, brown sugar, cinnamon, prunes, and apricots. Jim and I finally found the dried apricots last night. The brown sugar is dark brown. My New England heritage demands that slight molasses taste, even if molasses was once part of the infamous triangle trade of slaves, rum, and molasses. Something to ponder during the coming Holy Week.

I grate a little orange zest over the mixture. It's my secret ingredient. I pour the melted Smart Balance over everything. The tzimmis comfortably fills the disposable roasting pan I've purchased for it. Jim smiles at my reasons for not using butter: surely there will be a brisket and you can't have dairy and meat at the same meal. "These people aren't Orthodox," he laughs. I'm thinking that even the non-Orthodox might observe Kosher at holiday time. I'm a little worried about the

2 percent dairy that I discovered on the Smart Balance label this morning. I think Leviticus says less than 1/64th dairy is OK. Besides, if people eat something unawares, does that count as a transgression? Let it be on my head.

A good Christian thought. Sins on somebody else's head. First, Jesus died for our sins. Later Christians blamed the Jews for his death. If the death was foretold in scripture, doesn't that make the Romans and their Jewish flunkies the pawns of divine history?

I have a theory. I think the tradition of animal sacrifice was still lurking about the edges in those days, certainly among the barbarians who eventually became Christian. Jesus died because we were bound to kill off God-given goodness, that radical bearer of the plumb line. I am grateful for Jesus and what he taught us heathens. It's just that I think God forgave sins all along, if a person truly turned away from them.

The tzimmis is cooling on the porch now. Church is already in session. I shall get dressed and take a long walk on this beautiful spring morning. God is in His holy temple. I think the whole world is His temple. I really look forward to the first night of Passover. I shall enjoy the old story of Exodus, the lively conversations, and especially that moment when someone raises a wine glass and says, *"L'Chaim."*

ME AND MY CHURCHES
by Ruth Granick

I was hired as the professional singer in an Evangelical Lutheran church in Austin. That lasted until some of the volunteers learned to carry the alto line, then I became *de trop*.

I don't remember my first regular solo job. I'd sent a begging letter and my music résumé to every church within an hour's drive from home. My vocal coach told me to work on diction, since the words of any solo are the most important.

A church in a northern suburb needed a substitute soloist—their regular soloist was in show business and not available for the next two Sundays. The organist was wonderful, I chose a musically unthreatening piece, and after the service as I walked down the center aisle to leave, members of the congregation thanked me for a beautiful solo.

The organist gave me a solo for the next Sunday, asked me to look it over, and do it only if I wanted to. It turned out to be lovely. After that second service I asked, rather indifferently, whether he had composed the solo. He'd used a pseudonym on the score and, indeed, it was his. He then gave me a book of his compositions and asked me to be their permanent substitute soloist. He said their regular soloist was in theater and out about half the Sundays each year. I told him I really wanted a permanent position. He expressed his regrets and said their regular soloist refused to sing any of his compositions!

A church in Elmhurst hired me. At that time I was terrified of standing in front of people and singing. I used a tranquilizer that my doctor told me many professional musicians took. The organist-pianist was a young, very pretty person who wanted to be a nightclub pianist. She came to church in curlers, thinking that she could not be seen through the louvers that fenced in her instrument. She could! After each service she sight-read next week's piece. She was a good sight-reader, as well as she should have been, since she never practiced during the week. What she saw was what we got.

That was where I learned a lot. During one service a woman collapsed in back of the congregation. A practitioner spoke to her, they listened quietly to the solo, then her brother was phoned and she was rushed to the hospital. Her brother, not a True Believer, was furious that she'd not been shipped off immediately for medical help. It was also at that church that one of the Readers spoke of having a cold. I knew they did not believe in illness and questioned her. She said, "We're not perfect yet, dear." Evidently they were not fiscally perfect either. They later closed the church, selling their building to the city which, I was told, made it their city hall.

Letters went out again, with my music résumé, all on very lovely, thickly textured, cream-colored paper. A Chicago church called me for an Easter service. The Head of the Music Committee gave me a solo but said I could do it or any other piece I chose. His song was banal, trite, pedestrian. I could imagine perpetrating it. At church, I sang something with most appropriate words and, again, non-threatening music. There was whispering and, at the end of the service, I was asked, very sternly, why I'd not sung what I'd been given. He'd had to apologize to his people for my choice, and we never met again. I auditioned in Maywood Park where, during the rehearsal, I broke off the rather high heel on one shoe. I did the service on my toes. I never heard from them—was I hired, was I not—later learned the church had been sold as the population changed.

Second Church in Chicago thanked me for my audition, said they'd hired a man since they'd always had a female soloist. I continued to send out letters and résumés.

How did I meet Kay Besold? What a fortunate encounter. She and her husband had left the large church in their town; they disagreed with something done there. The Besolds rented a small space alongside the Eisenhower, and installed an organ. She played, her husband read, and I was hired as soloist.

I was warned not to vocalize there before the service because I could be heard outside and neighbors must not be disturbed. Kay and

I became friends, she frequently invited me to lunch after service, and did very little proselytizing.

Ethel was part of our rather sizeable congregation. She was a very enthusiastic, loud hymn singer who sang totally off-key. My daughter, Sue, came to church once, to share a part of my life. I was so touched! I stood up to sing the first hymn, Sue's face turned ominous; she was obviously in a horrible mood. After the service, she explained that she had been trying not to giggle at Ethel's sound.

Some months later, Kay told me they would not be entertaining for a while. Actually, her husband had had a stroke. They gave up the church, and studied and prayed for his recovery.

Years later, I auditioned at a very large church, a typical Christian Science building, on Logan Boulevard. For more than a month I heard nothing, then came the Letter. They had sold their church; much of the congregation had moved elsewhere. They'd moved into their reading room and wanted me as their soloist.

I signed the contract saying that I don't smoke or drink. I put away the long dress I'd worn at services in larger churches, and went through my repertoire. By this time I no longer had a vocal coach and was totally on my own, since my voice teacher was not only not interested in my church solos, she really hated them.

First Reader was a warm, lovely lady. I always vocalized before the service, during the drive to church. Once I totaled my car and I had to take public transportation. First Reader agreed with me that vocalizing in the CTA was not appropriate. She invited me to her home, where I practiced. How generous of her!

The Head of the Music Committee was very conservative in her tastes, and once in a while vetoed a solo as "off the wall." Reminded me of Kay who, every once in a while, told me that the solo I'd chosen was "not appropriate for our church, dear." I finally realized that when she could not play a piece, that was her alibi.

Logan Square church's first organist was an arrogant young man who told me how to perform my solos, expected the rhythm to be exactly metronomic in each piece, forget about expression, meaning.

We sat in the back during the sermon and read. Most fortunately, he turned his pages quite loudly. After the service I was asked to be more quiet, as we could be heard in front. I ratted him out; he left.

Kim was a very personable young woman who played rather well, although at times she "sweetened" the accompaniment, turning rather expressive pieces into pap. After a while she became bored with the job. She would appear, she would not appear. I became used to practicing the accompaniment of hymns and of my solos, in case Kim did not show. She finally quit.

During this time, Hans worked at my church when he could. For his first appearance, he planned to play a Handel piece as his prelude. We got to church, he looked at the organ, called it a toy, said he could not play what he'd planned. The pedal board didn't even go one octave, both manuals were too short, and the stops did not work. But what a treasure he was. He played beautifully, accompanied sensitively. However, the church needed a permanent organist. Organist? No, they sold the organ and got an upright piano, which was a much better instrument.

I contacted DePaul's music school and got Natsuko, pronounced Notsko. She was very conscientious, dependable, but after a few years, she left and we got Russians. They were excellent musicians and delightful conversationalists, for the short time between rehearsal and service. They were too good, got better gigs, left.

I've been at my present church for about ten years, choosing appropriate solos and working on them. Lately I've been accompanying my solos, forced, therefore, to choose those with simple accompaniment.

Multitasking is fine, but I am not good enough to pay attention to the music for the left hand, the notes for the right hand, the vocal line, and the tiny Spanish words I've cut and pasted above each line. Oh yes, the congregation is now composed of folk from Central and South America. They hold down a few jobs each, not very well-paying jobs. They know some English, but don't have time to attend

ESL courses. We can converse in English, but they need the solos to be sung in Spanish.

I bought a "Spanish for Dummies." It comes with a CD, which I inserted into the proper computer slot. Nothing shows at all. I need "Computers for Dummies."

TRAVELS WITH ADELE
by Barbara Gazzolo

We were in Morocco, the first ones at the bus that morning.

"That's a killer shirt you're wearing," she said.

It was a favorite of mine though I was never quite sure what it meant, a black shirt with bold white letters. CARPE MAÑANA, seize tomorrow. For the lethargic it might mean to do it tomorrow. For me, and clearly for Adele, it meant to make the most of life now.

But for Adele it meant even more than for me. Her beloved husband, Sam, was not well, and this trip to Morocco was just one part of their decision to seize today and, yes, tomorrow while they could.

When I returned home to Chicago, I sent her a shirt like mine. It was meant to be our love of life uniform. But when they got home to California, Sam had a stroke and died.

Though we had just met and barely knew each other, I suggested that she and I meet with two other new friends, Harry and Kirsten, in Colorado. This came to be a tradition. It also began our time as travel mates, seizing together today and tomorrow.

I can still remember our breakfasts with the Van Loons, morning coffee and Danish cheese and dark bread as we talked together of the state of our world, our nation in particular. I remember Adele knitting a little cap for my new granddaughter. I remember her waiting for me at the gate of many different airports, often wearing the black shirt with our slogan, *carpe mañana*. I remember her amusement at my reaction to my first earthquake in Peru. It's only a four or five she said to comfort me—the girl from Illinois. I remember her coming from California to care for me when I broke my ankle.

Together we would see Machu Picchu, Angkor Wat, Hanoi, Rajasthan, Moscow, Warsaw, Rome, Padre Island off of Texas, and the wondrous quetzal bird of Costa Rica, never mind the Chicago architectural boat ride on a windy day. Wherever Adele was, she engaged fully with the place, with the people, as a teacher always eager to mentor the young she encountered.

Once we had taken an Elderhostel bird-watching trip to Texas and actually spotted a whooping crane on a deserted island—deserted but for a sinister coyote in search of dinner. That night, stretched out on our prim Holiday Inn beds watching TV, the news broke on Monica Lewinsky.

"I don't believe it," she said. "The Republicans are just trying to get him."

"Don't be too sure," I warned. "Those things happen with him."

"No," she insisted. "I feel I know Bill Clinton. He feels almost like a brother or a friend. He wouldn't do something like that."

I shook my head and shut up.

Months later, I was in a Moscow hotel, showering after days on the Trans-Siberian so-called Express. Harry, Kirsten, and I had seen a lot of Russia a little bit at a time. As I stepped from the shower wrapped in a towel, the door opened and Adele walked in. Sort of fresh from London, she threw several newspapers on the bed and hugging me, apologized.

"You were right about Clinton. Just look at these newspapers," she said. You have to love someone who can admit with such grace that they were wrong.

We celebrated my birthday in Moscow, moved on by that same weary Express train to Warsaw, ate some great borscht there, and flew to Rome to celebrate the Van Loons' fiftieth wedding anniversary in an old castle. Style all the way.

No adventure could end without the inevitable question. Where are we going next year? After all, we meant to seize tomorrow, and we did. I can see her now in her tan safari vest with the black cat pin on the front pocket, posing in front of one historical site after another—always the safari vest and the black cat, but in the background one wondrous site after another, from Machu Picchu to the Taj Mahal.

After Hanoi and Cambodia we set our sights on India, northern India. Overseas Adventure Tours offered a good trip there and we signed on for the next January.

I don't quite remember when or where she shared her news, but between Hanoi and India, Adele told me she had been diagnosed with cancer.

There we were in New Delhi, roommates as always, and I would not have known she was ill except she had lost a few pounds. It was a great trip, and my friend was all there every inch of the way. Our new friends before parting for home asked us, "Where are you two going next?"

We were pleased with their question and thought a bit before answering. What would a year bring was left unsaid between us. Then we told them that we were in the mood for some nature and would head for Costa Rica. And they signed on for it too, the next January, we promised.

When Adele and I signed on for Costa Rica, I kept my doubts to myself, and in our phone calls across the country would speak excitedly of the birds we would see. But I would also ask how she was doing out there and decided to travel in October to see for myself. I half expected to care for her, but should have known better. She had arranged that we meet with friends of hers, go out to dinner, even go to San Francisco one evening. It was a totally fun time and she sent me home, as she always had, with lemons and guava from the trees in her back yard. Very little was said about the cancer, but her wardrobe was a new one and two sizes smaller than in India. We parted with plans to meet at the hotel in San José.

On January 10, 2008, Adele and I flew on separate planes to meet in San José. She had arrived first and, as I went up in the elevator to our room, I felt anxiety. She had announced she had yet a newer wardrobe, this one in size four. In Viet Nam she wore size twelve. In India she wore size eight. In Costa Rica she wore size four.

I knocked on our hotel room door and there she stood, smiling broadly, her arms open for a welcome hug. There wasn't that much to hug, but her spirit was size twenty-four.

There were days when she would choose an afternoon nap over an outing. Most nights she would take a sleeping or a pain pill and sometimes both, but when she got on the bus in the morning you would never know she wasn't 100 percent there, because she was. When we were alone in our rooms, I would have been open to hearing her talk about her cancer, but that wasn't her choice except one time after a bad dream.

Adele was too busy seizing now even as tomorrow became less likely, and we did get to see what we had set out to see in Costa Rica. Up in the mountains that run like a backbone down the center of the country, we saw our quetzal bird, the birder's dream. It's a splendid creature of scarlet-and-blue and emerald green, about a yard long and extremely rare. On our outings around the hostel where we stayed, we saw four of them, and close-up too. Their slim emerald tails, as long as the bird itself, blowing delicately in the breeze. No wonder the kings used their tails as part of their crown. No wonder they were hunted almost to extinction. But we saw our stunning quarry perched above us in the trees and our quest was complete. Now we could board the bus and return to San José for a last night there.

We were having a farewell dinner and Adele was putting on her new size-four ensemble. At dinner that night someone was talking about difficulty falling to sleep.

"I have no trouble falling asleep," I put in. "When you have a roommate who likes to discuss the Truman doctrine, it's no problem at all."

Rising to my prod, Adele rose from her chair and responded fiercely, "All right then. This will be the last time I travel with you."

The friends understood the exchange, both its playfulness and its courage. They laughed and remembered.

The next morning, we shared a last breakfast of coffee and fruit and breads, and the bus drew up to take some of us to the airport. I had passed around a note from Adele telling everyone she didn't want to say good-bye—so long would do nicely.

By the bus door I gently hugged my friend and chose to say, "It's Obama on Super Tuesday, you know," rather than "so long."

She nodded, and I boarded the bus. I watched friend after friend hug her. Her plane was leaving last.

As our bus pulled away, I watched Adele turn and walk slowly towards the hotel entrance. She was wearing, as she always did, her safari vest though I couldn't see the black cat pin on its front pocket. She knew it was over now, and there was both courage and weariness in each step she took.

I called California the next day to see how her trip home went. "Just fine," she said, and told me how her girls had welcomed her and that she was unpacking and going to do some laundry.

A couple of days later, I called to check in with her and was told by her daughter that she was in her bed, though she would get up to greet and visit friends who came to call.

That whole week home, I was getting ready for my knee surgery and called less then I might have. A week and two days after coming home, Adele voted absentee ballot for Obama from her bed. Two days later, she met individually with each of her three beloved grandchildren, taking each into her bed to talk and to hold once more. The next day, Sunday, she fell asleep and, just as she had told her family she would do, she died on Tuesday, Super Tuesday.

Adele knew what it was to seize tomorrow and even as she lay dying, she fiercely took tomorrow in her embrace.

WHOSE STUFF IS THIS ANYWAY?

by Sarah Mirkin

I am selling my wonderful, 115-year-old Victorian house in Evanston, where I have lived for twenty-two years. In fact, I have sold it and now am going through the exercise of downsizing, since I am moving into a condo that has about one-third of the space of the house. This house was packed to the gills when my husband, Bernard, died in 2007, four years ago. Since the house is large, and we had a complicated family life, everyone deposited things here over the years. All the nooks, crannies, shelves, hidden cabinets, bookcases, file cabinets, old trunks, closets within closets, and hollow window seats on the third floor were stuffed with stuff. Squirrels got to some of it, and we didn't notice for months.

I want to blame part of the accumulation on Bernard. He could not throw anything out. When we moved here from Minneapolis, I came first because I took a job I could not refuse. I would work here four days a week and then return to Minneapolis where I would painstakingly sort through things and put them out for trash pickup. As soon as I left Minneapolis for the four-day work week in Chicago, Bernard would restore all the things I had trashed, putting them back in their place. I gave up arguing with him. So we moved here with everything and then threw out most of the things I had tried to discard.

Bernard's belongings consisted of many items from his boyhood family and many more things, which he and his first wife, Phyllis, had acquired over their long marriage. Phyllis had grown up poor in a tiny flat in the South Bronx, so she liked acquiring things. Her acquisitiveness and his inability to discard mounted up. His two grown daughters had left many of their childhood possessions behind. Those also came with us to Evanston. After his death, I was asked to clear out his office. There, I found many things I had thrown out over the years of living in Evanston. So I got to throw them out twice. After his death, I wanted to surround myself with what was his and what was ours. I also found it very satisfying to give something of Bernard's to someone who loved him and who mentioned some item in the house. It meant a lot to that person and a lot to me to turn that item into a gift in remembrance of him. That practice continued over a year or more, but the house never looked any less full.

I had acquired many antique pieces from my family, who also liked to keep things. My children, too, had left many of their belongings in the house, planning to pick them up on some visit. And of course there were the things which Bernard and I brought back from numerous trips to rather exotic places. We were so busy with our professional lives that we seldom thought about discarding some of what had gathered here. About five years ago, I made a vow to myself and to Bernard that if we brought anything into the house, something else would have to go out. That was a sad little effort to acknowledge that we had far too much packed into this place.

Then Bernard died and left me as sole owner of all our earthly belongings: car, boats, books, artwork, china, silver, rugs, beds, records, CDs, furniture from any age—all of it. He even bequeathed his frequent-flier accounts to me. In a way, it was a loving and generous gesture. In another way, knowing Bernard as I did, he was saying to me, "NOW you can get rid of it. No one will stop you." And I was tempted to begin tossing indiscriminately. Why not make a clean break of it and let go of belongings without regard to their history?

However, there were people in line with their various expectations. Bernard's two daughters, my three children, his sister and her children, his friends, my friends. I was being approached in all manner of ways from all directions.

Shortly after his death, I had a gathering of Mirkins at the house to recognize Bernard's passing. Mirkins came from all over. They don't get along well enough to gather together for any positive reason. But for a death, they show up. Mirkins are not religious, so the gathering had no spiritual content, which left the afternoon open to any number of past resentments. After several decades of living with Bernard, I understood that the Mirkins never solve problems among themselves. They fertilize them with rancor. And the problems thrive.

I had been thinking that perhaps I should spare myself and others the chore of selecting items, wrangling over them, bringing up past episodes. All this was legally mine. Perhaps I should select what I really need and sell or toss all the rest of it. That would be clean, even-handed, and even honorable in a cold kind of way. If I was going to acknowledge the legal right to everything but abandon the consequent right to get rid of it all, by what method was I going to begin distributing?

There was the issue of need. I could determine what all these people needed and then see to it that those things were delivered to them. The problem with this method of distribution was that the needy didn't want these things. In fact, in most cases their neediness was my idea, not theirs. They simply didn't want what I felt they needed. My son Jacob told me that the only reason he would take anything was because I wanted to get rid of it. That idea was quickly put to rest when I discovered what it would cost to ship anything from Evanston to Austin, Texas.

I searched further for the most ethical way of distributing things, once I had decided against the legal route of possession and elimination of all goods. Need clearly was not the determining principle. Perhaps I should just lay everything out over a weekend and invite the five children, mine and his, to come and select. That idea had a delicious Charles Addams quality to it, since the two sets of children dislike each other. But that wouldn't work. My children would hold me in contempt for creating such a scene and wouldn't show up.

I was getting plaintive little e-mails from Bernard's younger daughter, laced with lists of items that she felt attached to, things she had grown up with. I couldn't deny that attachment; in fact, I honored it. His daughters were trying to hold on to him through things they remembered from their childhood. So I sent them what I could send and then invited them to the house one Sunday in April to carry off the things they had identified and I had agreed to give them.

They arrived with a large SUV—one might call it a small van—and proceeded to load up. I had put everything they wanted in the front hall, hoping to forestall their prowling through the house for other goods. One daughter wanted to look at some of the art books she remembered as a child, so I led her up to the third floor and left her there leafing through books and gazing at images. I told her she could take what books she remembered. I went back downstairs and helped the others carry things to the car. Bernard's younger daughter came down with a load of books in a large bag, the last things were carried out, and off they went. I went to the third floor to discover that several items had disappeared from her father's desk, and a few other books which were not in the "art section" had also vanished. I have no doubt that she considers those items hers, and she believed that she was simply reclaiming what was hers. Well, so much for the ethical stance. I felt duped and stupid for setting myself up for that one.

I will attempt to furnish my new space so that it reflects my aesthetic preferences, and I will continue to refine this collection by keeping only those things which I think are beautiful. This gives my collection coherence and wholeness. Hopefully it will also speak to people who visit me. My new home will become a memoir of objects. Refining this definition of taste means that some things must go, but making aesthetic decisions will allow me to give away what is marginal. My decision to use the aesthetic standard for keeping things leaves the law, and passivity in the face of greediness, and muddled ethical decisions behind and brings self-identification forward. The stuff becomes something abstract as a whole, but it is still personal. When I am dead and gone this effort at self-definition will dissolve. What I have gathered to make a statement will disappear in who knows what directions. Whose stuff will it become anyway?

DURIAN
by Stella Mah

What is Durian? Who is Durian? Is it some famous Armenian we should know? Does the word sound strange? Well, if you saw a durian you would think it looked strange, and if you were close enough to see a durian you would undoubtedly smell it. It's got a skunk-like odor, which you would never forget.

Durians are grown in Southeast Asia, especially in Malaysia. The durian tree is very tall, well over sixty feet before it bears fruit. A mature tree can be over a hundred feet tall. A tree that bears good fruit is prized by the owner and guarded, night and day, close to harvest time to prevent theft. It is not easy for a durian thief to steal the fruit. He must be able to climb the tree to the very top where the fruit hangs by stems as thick as a man's thumb. The fruit, about the size of a pineapple and weighing between six and eight pounds, hangs from the limbs away from the main tree trunk, thereby offering another challenge to the thief. Still, thieves have stolen the prized fruit successfully. As though the fruit knows its own value, it grows a thick shell with powerful spikes all over its surface for protection. To hold it, one had better wear thick leather gloves, as the spikes can pierce cotton ones.

The durian has to be pried open at the base by a wooden implement, revealing segments of nested fruit, each having a stone in the center. The texture is like heavy custard, and it is very sweet, with its own inimitable flavor. Usually one eats it out of one's hand, as durian lovers cannot wait to taste it. The odor permeates the whole person, like garlic, exuding from pores and breath.

And now we come to the scent. For those who love the fruit, it is equivalent to Chanel #5, but those who do not love the fruit compare its odor to rotten meat. One can argue that it is perfume or that it is foul smelling, but one cannot argue about its power. It can be smelled blocks away. Neighborhood fights may ensue between the fruit lovers and the fruit haters.

As with all things that elicit strong feelings, there is a superstition that lovers of the fruit will return to the area no matter how far they may roam. My parents took to the fruit right after their arrival in Singapore, where they both lived out their lives. Although I partook of the fruit in my early years, I cannot say I either loved it or hated it.

I remember one year my parents invited Richard, my husband, our son, Chris, and myself to a Malacca seaside resort for a week. On the way from the airport to the resort, our taxi driver suddenly veered off the main road. We thought we were being abducted. But no! He had noticed a sign about a mile back announcing that durians were for sale. That particular farm produced the best fruit around, and he had to buy some or he could not go home to his wife that evening. He bought so many durians that he crammed them into the car trunk with our suitcases. In just the thirty minutes it took us to get to the resort, the odor transferred to our luggage. We walked into the lovely lobby trailing the signature scent with us. Besides being embarrassed, we had to do two loads of laundry right away.

Richard, my husband, who was not from Singapore, could not understand the passion this ugly fruit elicited. The first time he tasted it, he quickly spat it out. I guess he proved the superstition was correct, as he never returned to Singapore.

THE BEST TIMES OF OUR LIVES
by Lou Polley

The nest was empty! The children had flown away. Bill had retired from his desk job and was spending lots of time at the farm he inherited from his father.

I was still teaching, but was looking for second-career options when I retired. We went to herb and organic farming conferences regularly and began to grow basil plants of all kinds: tiny-leafed Greek basil in olive oil cans; purple ruffled-leaf basil; soft-leaved Italian basil, perfect for pesto and just becoming popular among chefs and foodies. Soon we had so many plants we didn't know what to do with them. Mrs. Thrifty decided it would be fun to sell them. I called on several chefs, who gave me orders for plants and cut basil leaves, and voilà, a business was born! We named it Gourmet Gardens and expanded our products to include a little-known green called arugula, which was a hard sell at first because few people knew about it. But once tasted, became a hit!

We were invited to bring our basil and arugula to the Best of the Midwest food show held annually at Navy Pier. We expanded again to include mizuna, unusual lettuces, heirloom tomatoes of every size and color, cippolini onions, golden beets, squashes of all varieties, many with their blossoms still attached. Long before they became a popular item at the supermarkets, I put together bags of mixed salad greens topped with pretty, tasty nasturtium blossoms. Eventually we supplied several high-end restaurants with our produce, selling what was left to several local farmers' markets, including Evanston's.

The first time we brought our produce to the Evanston market, I spread out the green-and-white tablecloth that I had used at the Best of the Midwest food show and began to arrange my greens artistically. "What ya doin? Fixing lunch?" quipped the Michigan fruit grower next to us with unmistakable sarcasm in his voice. Several weeks later a few other tablecloths appeared in other booths. By the end of the season, even the Michigan fruit grower was "fixing lunch."

At first it was strictly a Ma-and-Pa operation, but soon our children and grandchildren joined in the venture whenever they could. Retired? We never worked harder in our lives nor enjoyed ourselves more.

MY NAME IS ALBERT
by Barbara Gazzolo

Dressed in my Sunday clerics, I locked the front door and headed for the car. It was early and I needed to get to church in time to be ready for the first service. As I was opening the car door, a man on a bicycle swooped up beside me.

"Can you give me a little money?" he asked. "I'm hungry and that guy on the corner wouldn't give me a dime."

There I was, dressed as a clergy. How could I turn him down? I reached into my coat pocket and handed him a bill. He rode off and so did I.

If I thought that was that, I was deluded. Within a few days he reappeared on the front stoop, rang the bell, and asked for more money to get something to eat. He was quite thin, I noticed. He was in fact handsome. What didn't register at the time was his intensity. "I've just been released from prison and can't find work," he told me.

I'd done some work with prisoners and could imagine how hard it was to reenter society. "What's your name," I asked. "Tony," he answered.

"You look cold. I have a hooded sweatshirt. Would you like it?"

He nodded. Sweatshirt on, a couple of dollars in his fist, he went down the steps and rode off on his bike.

I saw a lot of Tony after that, you can be sure. On Thanksgiving he appeared at the door and, with overstuffed turkey and family at the table, I could hardly deny him money to buy something to eat. Occasionally he would bring a little gift, a small box of cookies, a pair of gloves.

As time went on, I found myself getting frustrated that he had not yet found work. A couple of times I had hoped he would get a job with a moving firm, but there was always some reason. One day he asked for bus fare. He had to go to Iowa, he told me. Good, I thought to myself, and gave him the thirty-five dollars.

Just as I had hoped, he was gone for a while, a month maybe. Then he was back again on the porch asking for some money to buy something to eat. He still looked thin and I handed him lunch money.

Then, for one whole week, he did not appear; and another week, no Tony. I began to feel freed. Months went by and I forgot what it was to hear the doorbell ring and see his weary face at the door.

I was driving down Dodge Street in Evanston one spring day and, pausing at a corner, saw a man on the sidewalk smiling at me. It was Tony, hardly recognizable because he had gained about thirty pounds. His face was fuller and the intensity was gone.

He waved and I stopped.

"I've been in Iowa," he said. "Went to the Salvation Army out there to get help kicking my drug habit. Now I'm getting a job out there."

"What brought you back here, Tony?"

"I needed to get my birth certificate. Then I'm going back."

"Hop in. I'll take you into town."

It was a quick ride from Dodge to Ridge Avenue. I stopped alongside the road and he opened the door to leave. As he did so, he turned and looked at me.

"My name is Albert," he said.

THE AMERICAN DREAM TURNED RANCID
by Mary Lee Maloney

Looking back on my life, it occurs to me that my parents weren't half bad. Many have been much worse. That said, I wonder how they could be caught up so completely in the American Dream when it costs us so much? I mean, who would trade evenings together as family for a beautiful Drexel cherrywood coffee table? Not a good trade, to me.

Yet, the longer my mother did without her traveling husband and her daughter did without a father, the more it seemed that things had to fill in for loneliness and loss. The Drexel coffee table was more than a table. It had the burden of symbolizing our ascending social status and, at the same time, compensating for a devalued self, a devalued marriage. That marble-topped coffee table in front of our humble couch was expected to make up for a missing dad, home only to repack his bags and hit the road once more. It was a dreadful cycle of his working harder and harder to make money as we bought stuff to compensate for his absence.

And while we're at it, we ought to replace that old couch for a fancy new one to match the Drexel. The cost of a new couch might put daddy and hubby away on the road a bit longer, but never mind, if we can just get ahead of the gang, prove our worth with our growing collection of things.

Our American Dream was off track. For some who do not take it to extremes, substituting things for solid loving values, the Dream lives. But for us, it was a sort of piranha taking a bite out of a family, then another bite and then another. A Dream misunderstood. Before you knew it, Ralph Waldo Emerson's wry observation made sense: "Things are in the saddle and ride mankind," he wrote.

My father was an intelligent, sensitive man. He had his blind spots and problems, as we all do, but wouldn't you think he'd be able to access that the longer he was away, on the road, the less he would see his wife and little girl? Couldn't he see that the loneliness of driving through the South was driving him to drink? But then there were the bills to keep up with. And Dad was more than a little compulsive. He kept every check in numerical order, from years back, in a bevy of shoeboxes up on his closet shelf. His daughter knew that was a little strange when she was only seven. Kids know.

Oh well. They meant well. They meant so well. My mother started off the marriage dutifully filling up her little wooden recipe box. Everything in order, aesthetically written out on little cards, kept in place within each category. Perfection is what these two strove for.

My father, fresh out of Notre Dame, was aiming for the top of the Electrola Company. He had a chance at the golden ring of success. His family had been Depression-era neighbors of the president and knew the family well. Perhaps this deluded him. My father may have thought to himself, "If I can just get a few more years of tremendous output, much like a racehorse in its prime, maybe that will do it. I'll be able to relax in style, I'll have it made for myself and for my family. Wife will be happy. Daughter will have the best of everything. Best of all, momma, Mighty Mida, as they called her, will be proud of her son. Graduate of Notre Dame. VP of Electrola."

But it was not to be. The trouble was that the needs of my mother, my father, and of me couldn't be met by tables and couches. Our needs were for basic security, love, and belonging. These unacknowledged, unmet needs coursed through our psyches putting lie to our American Dream. Looking back on it, I cannot believe that my mother could pack us up after four years here, leaving home in Chicago for hot, faraway Dallas. Once there, she began collecting large spiders in plastic containers to show my father after his long trips as regional salesman in the South.

Then, after only one successful year in Dallas, Electrola moved us, the Bob Hennessey family, up to Nashville, where Mother began collecting spiders again. I was only glad spiders were not as large as they had been in Dallas. Mama could be preoccupied with moving, redecorating, and with her appearance, but at least she would not likely die of an arachnid spider bite in Nashville.

I am almost sixty now and, as I look back at my parents in their twenties and thirties, I can see how it all happened. The implosion of this American family was inevitable. The Dream loomed too large back then. It was almost a directive rather than a dream for a young, well-educated, attractive couple coming from upwardly mobile families, one Irish, the other German and English. The fifties and sixties were boom years and everyone seemed to be on steroids trying to get ahead. The martini business lunches took their toll just as did all the time Dad spent away from us on the road. The center could only hold for so long.

After only two years in Nashville, Electrola had new plans for my father, a new move for my mother and me. This time we were to move into a brand-new house in a brand-new suburb of Chicago, called Westchester. As an eight-year-old kid, I had no realization of what this kind of unsettlement could be doing to my mother, but I did notice that Mom had begun to imbibe quite frequently from the tall, narrow, green glass decanter filled with sherry.

Things had become frayed between my parents in Nashville. Things began to unravel in Westchester. As an eight- or nine-year-old I enjoyed catching garden snakes with neighboring kids in our newly dug-up backyards before all of the pipes were put in. I loved having the Barnum and Bailey Circus come set up tent at the end of our nascent suburban street. But I knew in my perceptive child's spirit that the end was coming. The end of our little family was coming. I used to go off to a playground, nearby, as the sun was going down. I would play on the swings and slide with the darkening cool sky around me. Like a young cat I felt I needed to be alone in my painful knowledge. There was no way I could share it with other kids. There was no way to put it into words.

STUDS TERKEL
by Diane Ciral

Studs Terkel, author of many oral histories including the Pulitzer Prize-winning *The Good War* and host of the acclaimed radio show on WFMT, Chicago's fine arts station, became our neighbor when he and his wife, Ida, bought a house down the street from us on Castlewood Terrace.

Studs was most definitely a man of the people. Each morning, he would walk to the corner to catch the bus, a pile of books under his arm. I remember a day when I was digging in my garden when Studs passed my fence mumbling in a low voice. I thought nothing of it until it happened often enough to arouse my curiosity. When I finally asked him what he was mumbling, he replied that it was his way of rehearsing for his talk show that day.

Our block had open-house parties with Glogg and Swedish meatballs every year. One New Year's Eve, we were snowed in and I invited all the neighbors to celebrate at our house. Studs, as usual, held court. He recounted scene-by-scene Charlie Chaplin's film *Limelight*, which Shev and I had just seen. Although Studs hadn't seen this movie in years, he remembered it as clearly as if he had just seen it.

One day, Ida called Shev to help her with something in their house. He came home with a big grin on his face. In the basement, hanging on the clothesline, Shev had spotted seven identical red-and-white checked shirts, Studs's signature attire along with his ubiquitous red socks. When Studs was notified that he had won the Abraham Lincoln Award, he was told that he would have to wear white tie and tails. Although he agreed to concede to this custom, he appeared at the gala wearing red socks.

The Chicago Historical Museum wanted to publicize an upcoming exhibit about the history of puppets. As public relations director, I asked Studs if he would interview Burr Tillstrom, creator of a beloved program called *The Kuklapolitan Players*, which appeared daily on NBC television.

Among the cast of characters were bulb-nosed Kukla, a likeable and earnest fellow; Ollie, a dragon with a marshmallow heart and a single oversized tooth; floppy-eared Fletcher Rabbit; high-strung Madame Oglepuss, garbed in her usual black dress, white gloves, and long pearls; and Beulah Witch, with her crooked nose and black pointed hat. The charming and seemingly naïve Fran Allyson played the human foil for their dramas. As a great admirer of Burr Tillstrom, Studs eagerly agreed to my request.

The day of the interview, I accompanied Burr to the WFMT radio station. We walked down the hall to a small studio with a large glass window revealing the sound booth, the engineer, and the station announcer. On the table in the center of the room were two microphones, one for Burr and one for Studs. After they took their seats, Studs, with his unmistakably craggy voice, began by asking where Kukla and Ollie fit into the world-at-large. Burr explained that Kukla, always on his right hand, symbolized "everyman," whereas Ollie, on his left hand, represented an offbeat character, sometimes sinister or gauche.

This being the era of the feminist movement, à la Betty Friedan, Gloria Steinem, and *Ms. Magazine*, the conversation turned to women's rights. Studs grilled Beulah Witch about what a woman's place was. "It's a wonderful thing for women," snapped Beulah. "It's time for women to get out in the world. Experience life as I do, flying around on my broomstick." At this point, Madame Oglepuss chimed in with a high-pitched operatic voice that women belonged in the home, raising children and taking care of their husbands. An argument ensued between the two "women," orchestrated by Burr's brilliant imagination and the remarkable flexibility of his larynx.

Sitting in the studio that day, I watched Studs Terkel and Burr Tillstrom together create a magical world of innocence, humor, and gentleness.

FATHER AND SON
by Dorothy Chaplik

Amos and I had known each other as teenagers. He had worked after school in his father's butter-and-egg store, where I frequently appeared with the shopping list left by my mother on the battered porcelain table in our kitchen with instructions to bring these items home for dinner without fail. A lifetime later, a handwritten list lying atop one- or two-dollar bills on my own kitchen table brings back my mother's commanding voice. "You hear me, madam? No dawdling after school. I want those groceries here when I get home!"

Sights and smells mingle as I remember standing in the middle of the Dorfman store, waiting for someone to say, "Well, young lady, what'll it be today?" His four years of seniority and extra height gave Amos the right to speak to me as if I were of a different generation, and the gap between us widened with his refusal to make eye contact. Back and forth, the sandy-haired Amos and his bald father paced the length and breadth of the store. Both were wrapped in long white aprons, their strings tied twice around the son, barely once around the rotund father, as they sliced wedges of golden butter and white cream cheese mounded on glass-enclosed counters, or reached into open barrels of tangy black and green olives, or selected from stacked shelves long loaves of rye bread redolent of caraway seeds. Each item neatly enclosed in freshly torn sheets of waxy white paper.

Amos and I had in common that, some twenty years earlier, our parents had emigrated from Europe and now were merchants on the same street in Chicago. Mr. Dorfman, with his Polish accent, had operated his thriving business in the same location for many years, surviving two wives in the process. His soft face and benign, tooth-less smile belied the tough disciplinarian within, who demanded that each of his seven children serve a permanent apprenticeship with him, making it unnecessary for him to hire outside help.

In contrast, my mother, Miriam Greene, was a relative newcomer to the community, working alone on a modest scale. Determined to be independent, a rarity in the 1930s for a woman approaching the age of forty with four children—three of them minors, she had chosen to divorce my jobless father and fend for herself. At a night school class, not long after her arrival in the States, she had learned the rudiments of reading and writing and soon was a fervent follower of romance novels. Later, when she decided to become a hairdresser, her reading skills enabled her to study and acquire a state license to practice beauty culture. Working in her chosen field was postponed when World War II was declared and, for a few years, she donned blue overalls to toil in a defense factory. Her generous earnings provided a down payment on a beauty shop of her own. By then, my brother had come home from the war and gone off to a university in the Southwest to study; I had reached majority and found a clerical job to support myself. Income from her small shop covered the needs of Miriam and my younger sister.

Mother was a beauty. Even in the sturdy black oxfords that were her only compromise with vanity, she caught the attention of passersby as she walked the few blocks between our apartment and her shop each morning and evening. With her dark, marcelled hair, fair skin, and deep blue eyes, she radiated an air of Irish ancestry, until she spoke and revealed unmistakable traces of a Russian-Yiddish accent. Miriam's accent was no barrier to the gentlemen who pursued her at the dances she loved to attend. Evenings our telephone rang often, followed by a string of social engagements. I remember the tall, handsome man in the ten-gallon hat who wanted to whisk her away to his Wyoming ranch, and the swarthy Italian with dreamy eyes who appeared at the door unannounced. After a few dates, Mother would lose interest. "Well, he's not Jewish," she would explain, shrugging her shoulders.

Not long after establishing her independent life, Mother came home from work one evening agitated, nearly hysterical. "The nerve of the man! That old goat!" The harangue continued as she removed hat and coat and paced back and forth. "Old enough to be my father!" At my urging, she finally submitted to a cup of tea and as we sat at the kitchen table, the facts slowly emerged. Mr. Dorfman, in his dark holiday suit, crisp white shirt, and black overcoat, had visited her shop that afternoon, daring to propose that my mother become his third wife. "That old geezer," she complained. "With his fat stomach and short legs! He shuffles around like a penguin. A dancing penguin."

I was puzzled by my mother's attitude. She was drawn to weekly dances at the Green Mill or the Aragon Ballroom, but inevitably rejected the men she attracted. Now a man of her own faith, and a merchant in good standing in the community, had offered his hand and her response was still negative. I asked, "Why be upset, Mama? Isn't a marriage proposal a compliment?"

Mother's Irish eyes turned cloudy and Russian. "What do you know of such things?" she said. "You're a child!" This last remark was delivered with dramatic disdain, despite my eighteen years. But a moment later she threw back her head of black, wavy hair and laughed, as the electric ceiling light flickered across the gold fillings in her teeth.

If Mr. Dorfman was injured by my mother's rejection, it was not fatal, and he soon found a willing bride closer to his own age. About this time, whether due to the change in his father's life I was never certain, but Amos escaped total commitment to the family business and enrolled at a law school, though he continued to work in the store in his free time. We met occasionally at the train station, on our way to or from Chicago's Loop, where I worked as a secretary during the day and attended art classes at night, and where his law school was located. As the train sped over the elevated tracks, we clung to straps suspended from the ceiling, conversation discouraged by the roar and screech of the wheels. If we found seats together, we routinely exchanged polite enquiries about the health of each member of our respective families before turning to our respective reading material.

Amos's usual tight reserve left me unprepared for the intensity of his reaction one evening when I unexpectedly described the art class I had just attended. I said, "It's always exciting to see the line of the model's body come to life on my drawing paper."

He said, "Art's an escape from reality! Take the law. That's about real life."

Later I learned not to stray in our conversations from the safe parameters of our respective families. He never mentioned friends, male or female, nor outside interests, and I decided he probably would pursue the bachelor life of a legal scholar and not imitate his thrice-wed father. It surprised me a few years later to learn that Amos had married, as I had. We went our separate ways and decades passed before we met again.

Amos's thick sandy mane had all but disappeared when next we saw each other, and my own dark hair was turning gray. Following the death of his wife and learning I had been widowed, Amos had contacted me. With none of the usual social amenities, his authoritative telephone voice kept our conversation brief and businesslike as he invited me to dine with him. Facing each other through bifocals across a restaurant table, I observed that the slim young man I had known in my youth had taken on the shape of his old father. We spoke of our parents. The elder Mr. Dorfman, now long deceased, had survived his third wife by several years. My mother, too, was gone, after a long and lonely life.

Sitting now at the restaurant table with Amos, I asked, "Are you aware that your father once proposed marriage to my mother?" A look of disdain spread across his usually placid face. He asked, "What would I know of my father's romantic life?"

I asked if his father's last marriage had been happy, and he replied, "Of course! His wife took care of him. Cooked his meals. Helped at the store."

Courtroom experience undoubtedly influenced the terse, abrupt manner of Amos's replies. And when he spoke of himself, he preferred monologue to dialogue, as if he were addressing a jury. Then, in a sudden shift of mood, he exclaimed, "I'm a wreck of an old man. Adrift and tired. My house, a mess. The mail, piling up. I don't eat properly." He stopped to spear large hunks of steak and fried potatoes.

Picking at my broiled fish, I followed his pause with a change of subject. Although he never asked, I spoke of my career as an art teacher and, with as much objectivity as I could muster, I described my two children and their work in the arts.

He replied, "What good is it to have children? They settle in other cities and leave you to face old age alone."

"We don't own our children, Amos."

"Rubbish. I would have forced my sons to study law and practice in Chicago,"

Suddenly, Amos tipped his head and looked directly at me. "You and I, we go back a long time," he said. "You still look good. Healthy." He paused for a moment and I could almost see his thoughts formulating around his house, his meals, and his mail. He began, "We're both alone now, you and I . . ."

Quickly I invented an expected telephone call of great importance, and brought the evening to an end. In the short walk to the car, I observed that Amos's extended girth, wrapped in a black overcoat, had given him a mincing gait. My mother's words came back to me. "A dancing penguin."

HYMN 663
by Penelope Whiteside

"Thou hast in grace my table spread secure in all alarms and filled my cup and borne me up in everlasting arms."

There are times when I feel enormously grateful. People don't always understand my sense of good fortune. After all, I have lost two wonderful husbands. It is true that there are gray days when I reminisce, sinking into feelings of sadness. Under cloudy skies I yearn for all the people who are now gone. I cry out against all the infirmities that threaten to take away even those I cherish today. Yet, just now it is sunny and cool. The blue sky spreads above the emergent leaves, the daffodils, tulips, and rhododendron. Tiny fists of lilac are waiting to extend their fingers. The rose bushes are thrusting forth, trying to catch up. My husbands would have been proud of my yard and garden. They made it possible. I am grateful for them.

Living in the present moment is what I've finally learned to do. Years ago, widowed for the first time, I took $7,000 out of my meager bank account, managed a three-week leave-of-absence from a job that paid only $22,000 a year. I was determined to join a mission group from across the United States and travel to India. I remember consulting some Native American medicine cards before I started: I drew an eagle and a raven.

"Eagle medicine is the power ot the Great Spirit, the connection to the Divine. It is the ability to live in the realm of the spirit, and yet remain connected and balanced within the realm of Earth," the eagle card read.

The message from the raven was more ambiguous. "Raven magic is powerful medicine that can give you the courage to enter the darkness of the void, which is the home of all that is not yet in form." A wild apprehension seized me. I was about to set forth on Air India. Did they even know how to pilot airplanes over there? I knew not another soul who would be embarking on this journey with me. Furthermore, as we flew over miles of brown desert—probably Iran—I imagined a crash in enemy territory.

Somehow, before one dawn on that trip, I found myself in a little boat on the mythical Ganges River. The small wooden boat was propelled by a slightly built walleyed Indian man. Funeral pyres lit up the shore, burning the devout Hindus who had come to the holy city of Varanasi to die. Men and women were bathing nearby. The women walked into the murky water in one sari and emerged wearing another. As I watched, I remembered the eagle and the raven. I had indeed entered another spiritual realm, full of darkness but also of transforming magic.

Elevated states of being don't last forever, of course. I returned from India to the same meager salary that barely covered my living expenses, and my savings account depleted by $7,000.

"I spent thousands of dollars to visit poor people," I liked to quip, back then. Yet, I felt renewed for all of that. Serendipity nudged its way into my vocabulary. The possibility of spiritual connection to all humanity and nature seemed palpable.

As I look back, I realize impulse has guided me well in the past. I married my first husband within a few months of meeting him. I welcomed two unplanned sons and, with them, a sense of adulthood. We bought our first house in a single afternoon—no contingencies there! Nursing school was another wild idea. I had majored in English and was supposed to be a teacher or librarian, wasn't I? Yet, nursing became another turning point. A sheltered young woman met real life. Surrounded by the ill and dying, I felt real and alive. A year after that fateful trip to India, I met my second husband and quickly married him.

All this makes me wonder about agonizing over anything. Fear holds one back. It tightens its grip when one thinks too long and hard about things. Fear projects the notion of failure, causing one to back off from even trying, from even protesting before turning down a certain path when that path is intuitively understood to be the wrong one.

On a recent birthday card to my granddaughter turning twenty, I wrote, "Don't be afraid to live!" I went on to tell her that "springtime" is such a lovely time of life. I've never talked to her before like that. I wonder what she thought of it? Never mind! I'm glad I said it. There were so many springtimes in the past when I wavered and retreated. This spring I am an elder, leaning down, if a bit arthritically, to savor all the precious shoots that the Earth puts forth. I am grateful.

I GROW OLD
by Ruth Granick

My mother used to recite poetry. One of her favorites was "The Love Song of J. Alfred Prufrock" by T.S. Eliot. "I grow old, I grow old, I shall wear the bottoms of my trousers rolled. Do I dare to eat a peach . . ." I grew to love it although, when I finally read the whole poem, I found it not entirely happy.

I grow old. My waist thickens, and my spine is shrinking. Decades ago I dated a man who lived in the John Hancock Building. We had dinner in Chinatown and then walked about. We came back to my place for coffee and he asked me to come and live with him. I wouldn't have to ever go back to work. He said, "Do you know why I want you to live with me? Because of this," and he pointed to my then-youthful throat.

That spot, too, is aging, and I am not pleased. I am glad that I will soon be eighty; I just don't want to look as though I were growing old. Some Hollywood actresses get their makeup tattooed on. I've always thought that was a super idea.

I was twenty-one when I got married. Every time we ordered drinks, I was asked for ID. I looked way under age. I was never flattered. It annoyed me. When my mother-in-law asked my age, and I said twenty-one, she replied, "Huh, you don't look bad for forty-one." I was annoyed that she was pretending to have misheard me, but I knew I was young and pretty, and her son had chosen me.

The other day I slipped on the ice at the Cos Building driveway, a medical building—what irony—and slammed down on my back and the back of my head. For a short while I had difficulty breathing, and my back and the back of my head hurt all that evening. Could a younger me have caught myself slipping and righted myself? I don't remember mincing along on the ice when I was young, stepping carefully, terrified of falling. Maybe there was no ice in those days.

My son, a doctor specializing in gerontology, tells me I can out-walk him. Yet, when I try one of those exercise-your-brain books, I find I can't even begin to understand some of the problems, let alone solve them. Was I always this way, or . . .

I don't want to go back there. My back was straighter, my face and throat unmarked by the years, I had more energy. But I understand myself more now. I understand what's happening to me and around me, and I can deal more sanely with it. The young are pretty, hand-some, slim, and straight-backed. They are also vulnerable, so inno-cent, so unknowing, and they have such a very, very long life ahead of them.

CONTRIBUTORS
Enid Baron, Co-Editor

Enid Baron is a clinical psychologist who returned to her first love, poetry, while she was writing her doctoral dissertation. Enid has served as vice-president of the Poetry Center of Chicago and co-editor of RHINO, a poetry magazine. She has taught poetry workshops in the public schools in Evanston, Illinois, where she lives. Enid has had a number of stories and poems published by literary journals. A collection of her poems was published by Riverrun Press under the title *Baking Days*. For the last four years, she has been teaching memoir writing at Evanston's Levy Senior Center. She considers this one of her most meaningful endeavors and hopes that *Weaving The Threads* will inspire readers to write their own memoirs.

Nancy Braund-Boruch

Nancy has had many careers, including college history instructor and administrator, banker, pension fund consultant, entrepreneur, and pastoral care minister. Nancy says all of these roles were exciting and fulfilling but the most sacred were her roles as hospital chaplain and as "minister" to the elderly and dying. Nancy lives in Evanston, Illinois and maintains a cabin in the woods in Pennsylvania and a timeshare in Santa Fe. She enjoys hiking, reading, and traveling and is currently working on two books, one prose and one poetry.

Dorothy Chaplik

A freelance writer and lecturer, Dorothy is the author of articles and books about the art of Latin America. Her original writing was inspired by a group of Hispanic children who expressed deep pride in paintings by Spanish artists when she guided them through the Art Institute of Chicago. In the process of writing, she travelled to Mexico and Puerto Rico and contacted artists and museums in other Latin American countries by telephone, mail, or online. This is her first venture into the fields of memoir and short story writing. A widow, she has two daughters and three granddaughters, all of them involved in the arts.

Diane Ciral

A former public relations executive, Diane Ciral is a civic activist. For many years she has chaired the Newberry Library's

Bughouse Square Committee, organizing its free speech festival each July in Washington Square Park. She is a founding board member of Friends of the Parks and sits on that organization's executive committee. In addition, she is a member of the International Woman Associates where she has chaired the Forum and the Woman Extraordinaire committee. She plays an active role in the Casablanca Committee of the Chicago Sister Cities International Program, which strengthens the bonds between the two cities through cultural, educational, and economic development projects and exchanges.

Barbara Gazzolo, Co-Editor

Born eighty years ago in a small Illinois town, Barbara was carefully reared to do well in school, be nice to her neighbor, eventually marry and, in turn, rear her own brood . . . all of which she did and then some. When the four children were half-raised, she enrolled in the Lutheran Seminary in Hyde Park. Eight years later, Barbara had her degree, was ordained, and spent twenty-four years as a pastor in Lake Forest. She had no idea where this would lead, and before she forgets it all, she is recording her adventures along the way. Her many contributions to the making of *Weaving The Threads* have been invaluable.

Ruth Louise Granick

Ruth Louise Granick's father wanted her named after Beethoven, but Ruth Ludviga, her mother, rescued her. Ruth enjoys classical music and knows that Johann Sebastian Bach wrote his music for her delight. She has sung in various choirs, including Rockefeller Chapel Choir. She now sings solo at church and is part of the Hinsdale Music Club, a group of professional musicians. Ruth walks her Boston Terrier or, rather, is walked by him. She lives in chaos, never having learned to make things neat. Ruth is blessed with two wonderful children. Dr. Aaron Lazar who, as a child, played the violin, is now a family practice doctor specializing in gerontology. Her daughter, Susan Darby, is an RN who has, in the past, played recorder, piano, guitar, and flute.

Beata Hayton

Beata Hayton attended the University of Chicago High School and College where she majored in economics. She says, "Why, I'll never know." After receiving her BA, she joined the City News Bureau in Chicago where she reported on local news. When World War II came to an end, women reporters were largely replaced by returning veterans, and Beata moved to New York City where she took a job fundraising for hospitals. Later, she worked in public relations for the National Council of Churches. Her lifelong passion for travelling to faraway places began during those years, when she travelled with her sister, Wilhelmina, and later with her husband, Bill. As a child, Beata grew herbs in her mother's garden and eventually in her own, becoming one of the founders of the first chapter of the Herb Society in Chicago. Some years later, the chapter produced *The Wild Onion Cookbook*. Another cookbook Beata was involved with for the Evanston Art Center was called *Creating Art*. A collection of recipes from Beata's family and friends contains recipes from all over the world. She recently completed a memoir intended for her beloved nieces and nephews and their offspring.

Pat Lee

Patricia Ann Lee was born and raised in Grand Rapids, Michigan. She has lived in Brisbane, Australia; Topeka, Kansas; and Denver, Colorado before finally settling in Evanston, Illinois. She taught in a one-room country schoolhouse at age twenty. Graduating from the University of Michigan, she taught high school English in both Standish and Case, Michigan. After a divorce and while raising her children, Pat obtained a Master of Social Work degree from Loyola University in Chicago. She then worked as a school social worker for nineteen years in Park Ridge. She's the mother of two sons and has five grandchildren.

Helen Levy

An offspring of parents born in Germany and the Fiji Islands, Helen grew up in an international home. Her parents sailed to New York in 1933, the day after their wedding. A decade later the welcome mat was out at their home in Chicago to extended family members fleeing the Holocaust. After college, Helen sailed with her husband to France, where his international career lasted for twenty-five years. They lived in Brussels, Norway, France, Spain, and England. One daughter was born in Oslo, the other in Paris. Helen's interest in genealogy motivated her to research her family history. She uncovered relatives from around the world: Australia, South America, Great Britain, New Guinea, and Zimbabwe. Helen's research goes back to the 1700s. On retirement, she and her husband returned to the States where they have new friends and have gotten involved in charitable work including The Selfhelp Home for the Aged.

Stella Mah

Stella was born in Shanghai, China at the beginning of World War II to professional middle-class Chinese parents. Her family went through tremendous upheavals, escaping to the interior of China for the duration of the War. They returned to Shanghai but left almost immediately to spend the next three years in Europe. Their return to China in 1949 coincided with the civil war between the Nationalists and the Communists. This forced her parents to leave China to settle in Singapore, where they lived until their deaths. For Stella's tertiary education, she went to England where she met her husband, Richard. They came to America and lived in several states, finally settling in the suburbs of Chicago where Richard became a distinguished professor of chemical engineering at Northwestern University and Stella received a degree in library science and took a position at School District 64 in Park Ridge, Illinois.

Mary Lee Maloney

Born in Chicago in 1951, she is the only child of Bob and Lenore Hennessey. Mary Lee and her mother moved to Dallas, Nashville, Michigan, Las Vegas—wherever Electrola transferred her father as a regional salesman. Her parents divorced when she was eleven. Her mother's second husband, Dr. James Clark Moloney, supported her in her travelling to Kobe, Japan, to attend high school when she was sixteen. After returning to the States, she enrolled at the University of Massachusetts in Amherst, following which she attended grad school at UC Berkeley. She worked with children as a teacher and as a reading specialist.

Sarah Mirkin

Sarah Mirkin never thought of herself as a writer, but she has flirted with the idea throughout her life. Reading was a great pastime when she was a child. Some of the books took on such vivid reality that appearing for meals seemed like the illusory world, and back she rushed to the real world of the book. Sarah took a bachelor's degree in English literature, taught English literature in a small college, and edited a series of literature textbooks. Now, in the later years, Sarah has a story she needs to tell about her late husband's fulfilling a dream of building a health clinic in western Tanzania. In doing so, she has begun to write other things, urged on by fellow burgeoning writers in a memoir class. Who knows where it will all lead?

Lou Polley

Born in May of 1930, Lou was truly a child of the Great Depression. As the youngest of four children, and being the only girl, she was spoiled and pampered. Her earliest heartbreak was losing her oldest brother in World War II. She was valedictorian of her high school class of 210 students. At age twenty she married Bill Polley, a first-generation Greek

American. Lou is the mother of three diverse and talented children and grandmother to five handsome grandsons and one beautiful granddaughter. After thirty years of teaching in Illinois public schools, Lou launched, along with her husband, an organic herb and specialty vegetable business called Gourmet Gardens. In January 2008, she suffered a severe stroke from which she is recovering.

Ruth Sherman

Ruth Sherman went around the block many times, seventy-nine to be precise. The first twenty were in the Bronx, and her writing in this anthology is a brief sampling of what they were like. Ruth has worn many hats and coats and even bikini panties, but what she has loved best is being a Bubbie (Grandma). Ruth lived in Evanston, Illinois, in a condo high-rise, and her floor-to-ceiling windows gave her a clear view of her world.

Deanne Thompson

Twenty-five years ago Deanne wanted to write a book. She had a great idea at the time and started to write it. After a few chapters she faced a writer's block and moved on to other things. Recently her nineteen-year-old granddaughter wrote a book called *The Eternal Kiss*. It was about vampires. Deanne remembers that when her granddaughter was younger, she always wanted to read Deanne's scary vampire books. Her first book has come out, and she has completed a second book and begun a third. Deanne's granddaughter has inspired her to find the unfinished manuscript she started all those years ago and, perhaps, she will finish it this time. Deanne says it may never meet a publisher's approval, but will be fun to try, and will help fill some of the empty hours in the days to come. Oh yes, one more thing. It is not about vampires.

Penelope Whiteside

Penny has lived in Evanston, Illinois, for almost fifty years. She has reared sons and buried two husbands there. Yet, that place of origin, New England, still shapes her sensibilities. And when people ask, "Where are you from?" she catches herself saying, "New England." Penny once imagined herself to be a barnacle! Growing up, she saw many of those minute crustaceans on seaside rocks. They clung to their chosen places as the waves crashed around them. Metaphorically speaking, there is something steadfast about them. Penny loves gatherings of family and friends, her nursing career, travel, the theater, music, serendipitous adventures. Mostly, though, she cherishes the peaceful times when she can sit on her own porch, perhaps looking out over the lilac trees bordering her garden and writing. Much like barnacles, she likes to cling to those things that endure.

"DEDICATED TO RUTH"
by Mary Lee Maloney

Am I going to turn away from those eyes and pretend I never saw them? Am I going to pretend I was just too dense to read more than sympathy from their looks? No, I'm not going to pretend, Ruth, that I didn't get some kind of message from you, as you sat across from me in memoirs class for more than two years.

You and I shared many similarities, though, of course, our stories were quite different. We were both only children born into abuse. In your case, it was fairly blatant. You had the disadvantage and advantage of knowing about it, early on. In my case, the abuse was far more covert, covered with something like "suburbanite" gentility. Who would imagine? Certainly not me, who wended her way for decades, as "Suzy Cream Cheese," as someone once called me. Blinder firmly fastened, lest I see life as less than ideal.

Your writing was raw, Ruth. I didn't like some of it. But, overall, I marveled at it. How could someone who had been through so much survive, as you did, with the aid of as little denial as you seemed to allow yourself? Did your clear inner vision come with age, or were you always so unsparingly committed to the truth about your childhood?

I will miss your scratchy voice, Ruth. How I now wish I had had the temerity to talk with you about more than how nice the garden was looking at the Levy Center. Why didn't I? You were the one person who not only shared with me much more of a past than I had allowed myself to see, but probably quite a bit of the present, as well, if the truth be told. We had many secrets, Ruth, just as all women do. I think those brooding eyes of coal under the pixie haircut possibly shared more with me than either of us cared to say.

We were unlikely soul sisters. One of us had one foot back in the first quarter of the last century; the other had spent her childhood suffocating behind appearances in the early fifties. You were a child in the steamy brewery of New York City at a time when fools literally weren't suffered kindly. An openly tough time. Not too much soft about it, depending upon the neighborhood in which you found yourself living. But a reality unrepentant of itself. A reality, glorious in its organic verisimilitude. The sights, the sounds, the smells of the Upper East Side, New York. Very little hidden there. This pungency worked its earthy way into your writing, Ruth. It hit us all in your sparse, often humorous descriptions, such as the odor of the streets when New York City Sanitation goes on strike.

Oh, Ruth, you had a lot to tell. You told it with an economic punch. I can't help wondering if you, like me, felt prevented, however, from telling most of it. We can only wonder what happened to you after the age of twenty. What were your early days in Chicago like? Tell more, Ruth. Tell more. But now you can't. Those broad lips, many times with a sort of wry smile upon them, have closed forever. No more stories from a different age.

Peace, Ruth. Be at peace.

26466240R00137

Made in the USA
Charleston, SC
08 February 2014